Dawson Trotman:
In His Own Words

Dawson Trotman:
In His Own Words

Compiled by Ken Albert,
Susan Fletcher, and Doug Hankins

NAVPRESS⬤

Discipleship Inside Out™

Discipleship Inside Out™

NavPress is the publishing ministry of The Navigators, an international Christian organization and leader in personal spiritual development. NavPress is committed to helping people grow spiritually and enjoy lives of meaning and hope through personal and group resources that are biblically rooted, culturally relevant, and highly practical.

For a free catalog go to www.NavPress.com
or call 1.800.366.7788 in the United States or 1.800.839.4769 in Canada.

ISBN-13: 978-1-61747-921-2

Cover design by Arvid Wallen

Some of the anecdotal illustrations in this book are true to life and are included with the permission of the persons involved. All other illustrations are composites of real situations, and any resemblance to people living or dead is coincidental.

Unless otherwise identified, all Scripture quotations in this publication are taken from The Holy Bible, English Standard Version (ESV), copyright © 2001 by Crossway Bibles, a division of Good News Publishers. Used by permission. All rights reserved. Other versions used include: the *Holy Bible, New International Version*® (NIV®). Copyright © 1973, 1978, 1984 by International Bible Society. Used by permission of Zondervan; and the King James Version.

Library of Congress Cataloging-in-Publication Data

Trotman, Dawson E.
  [Selections. 2011]
  Dawson Trotman : in his own words / compiled by Ken Albert, Susan Fletcher, and Doug Hankins.
     p. cm.
  ISBN 978-1-61747-921-2
  1. Christian life. 2. Spiritual life—Christianity. 3. Spirituality. I. Albert, Ken. II. Fletcher, Susan. III. Hankins, Doug. IV. Title. V. Title: In his own words.
  BV3785.T7A25 2011
  248.4—dc23

                                        2011025328

Printed in the United States of America

1 2 3 4 5 6 7 8 / 16 15 14 13 12 11

This book is dedicated
to the godly men and women
who have invested their lives
in discipling Christians
for the gospel,
for the Great Commission,
and for the glory of God.

Contents

Acknowledgments

In nearly twelve years of both graduate school and Christian ministry, I have purchased (and sometimes read) many books. I almost always enjoy reading the acknowledgments. No book, it appears, writes itself. No amount of reading, however, prepared me for the task of actually writing my first book. I am sincerely grateful to many people for their encouragement and support over the past several months.

In addition to making every document in their archives available to me, The Navigators and NavPress provided invaluable assistance with housing during two of my three research trips to Glen Eyrie. Their generous support gave me the freedom to write both this book and my doctoral dissertation (the writing of which I may no longer delay).

Susan Fletcher and Doug Hankins offered wise counsel and sound feedback on my sections of this book. I wish we all lived closer so that we could hang out and "talk Trotman" more often.

My two sons, Jerome and Caleb, showed patience far beyond their preteen years in putting up with my endlessly hogging the office and always being "busy working" through the long hours of reading and writing. Now that this book is done, I promise to let you use the office for at least one week (after that I have more work to do, sorry).

Thank you, Dr. Chuck Lawless and Dr. Timothy Beougher, for guiding me as I moved toward the study of Dawson Trotman, for allowing me the privilege of doing my PhD dissertation on this man, and for granting me the time away from that work to focus on this present book. I promise to "get down to business" on that project once again now that this one is completed.

My wife, Shawna, has had to endure being first a seminary widow and then a writer's widow for more than a decade. "Thank you" says far too little for all of her love and support through the times when she has had to do the work of two parents while also putting up with my endless verbal processing of what I am thinking and writing.

Above all, I give joyful thanks to Jesus, who is before all things and in whom all things hold together and without whom this work would be utterly void of meaning and purpose.

Ken Albert
Jeffersonville, Indiana
April 12, 2011

» » » »

On the occasion of my first book, I want to thank my large community of family, friends, and colleagues for their encouragement and support for this project. I first and foremost thank my Savior for speaking words of love to me during the hours I spent working on the book and for helping me know Him better. I am indescribably in awe of He who holds the universe together.

Thank you to Ken Albert and Doug Hankins for writing this book with me. You are both amazing men of God and a joy to work with. Here's to the future adventures of the Trotman Troika.

My colleagues at The Navigators have offered generous help and assistance. Paula Martin spent several afternoons typing the quotes that we extracted from Dawson Trotman's papers, proofreading my work, and fact-checking. I am grateful for her attention to detail. I thank Christopher Morton for his theological insights, for his unshakable belief in me, and for Friday-afternoon field trips. Donald McGilchrist has shared his vast knowledge of Navigator history with me, and I am profoundly grateful for this spiritual and academic mentor. I also thank Andy Weeks for allowing me the opportunity to serve The Navigators and for his forethought in preserving the ministry's heritage.

I thank the NavPress staff for their vision for this book. Thanks to our editor, Rebekah Guzman, and project manager, Tia Stauffer, for helping first-time authors understand the publication process.

I thank my parents, John and Ruth Fletcher, for their love and support. On the day I finished my final few pages of the book, my father drove across town to repair my gate that had blown over in a recent windstorm—just one example of their help and kindness.

The amazing women on my City Life Team are a blessing and delight. They endured my referencing Dawson Trotman's thoughts on many Scripture passages these past few months. Their prayers buoy me up, and their friendship and love for the Lord make my heart sing. Thank you, Becky Neumann, Jessica Chung, Natasha Curry, Brooke Zeller, and Lis Shackleford. I am especially grateful to Jessica for her thoughtful reading and editorial comments on my sections of the book.

Thanks to Dr. Annie Coleman, Dr. Glenn Sanders, Dr. Bill Mullins, and Anton Schulzki, who spent so much time helping me become a better writer and historian.

On a less serious note, I also wish to thank General William Jackson Palmer, founder of Colorado Springs and builder of Glen Eyrie. I am thankful that the Lord is allowing me to interpret your marvelous story. Rest in peace, General. Lastly, I thank Dawson Trotman for dedicating his life to helping others know Christ and for his words of insight contained in this book. Gentlemen, I look forward to meeting you both in heaven.

"Of making many books there is no end,
and much study wearies the body.
Now all has been heard;
here is the conclusion of the matter:
Fear God and keep his commandments,
for this is the whole duty of man."
Ecclesiastes 12:12-13 (NIV)

Susan Fletcher
Colorado Springs, Colorado
April 14, 2011

≫ ≫ ≫ ≫

I feel the need to put a disclaimer on my acknowledgments. While some of these phrases have often been hijacked by artists and carelessly used in the event of an award acceptance speech, they are nonetheless true representations of all that is within my inner being.

So here goes.

I want to first and foremost thank the triune God, who is the reason I live and move and have my being. Thanks to Ken Albert for his administrative gifting and persistence in bringing this project about and to Susan Fletcher, who had the vision and persuasion to make it happen. I would also like to thank the folks at NavPress and The Navigators for setting the pace in disciple-making in America.

Thanks to the kind people at Café Cappuccino in Waco, Texas, for free Wi-Fi, refills on loose-leaf English Breakfast Tea, and delicious breakfasts. Y'all helped fuel the inspiration to write. Thanks to the following music artists: Ryan Adams and The Cardinals, Sovereign Grace Music, Death Cab for Cutie, Derek Webb, and Arcade Fire, whose art spurs me on in writing.

I want to throw a shout-out to the irreplaceable community at Highland Baptist Church in Waco, Texas, who are the "Pauls" to my Timothy.

And a big thanks to my bride, Natalie Hankins, the real talent in our family. "You have bewitched me, body and soul."

Doug Hankins
Waco, Texas
April 13, 2011

Tues — SUN JUNE 24

Georgia, Lester, Lila, Bruce & I go to Glenn ranch where the Boys Bible Conference is to be held this year. We have lunch by a babbling brook & I pitch a tent that is to be head quarters at the Camp. Other years, because I was not able to arrive on the scene ahead of the boys, it has been always most been impossible to get caught up. I expect to overcome this difficulty this year. Late in the Aft. the rest go back and leave me in Camp. Just at dark the moon (full) came up & flooded the Canyon in a soft light that was Gorgeous. With the silence broken only by the stream I enjoy a wonderful Evening with the Lord. My heart is thrilled in the Secret of His presence. Sleep on the Ground.

MON June 25th

Up Early — Fix Signs for Camp — Lester arives early with Carload. The boys help get Camp ready Locate various Camps (8) The Camp this year had nothing ready. The boys will sleep out of doors. The meetings also will be held out of doors.
The Conference = June 25 — July 2

Mr. Corey of The S.S. Times was with us during the whole time. Speakers were Elmer Wilder, Bill Graves, Irwin Moon Smith, Adolph Fresius, Missionary from S.A. Don Milligan, Mr Corey, Dr Dickford & myself. 95 Boys — 11 leaders — Nurse. Some 35 boys professed Christ. As great a number yielded for Service. For details turn to files (3x5)" Boys Work) Lost 3 lbs on trip — long hours hard work but greatly enjoyed.

MON July 2 '34

Yokum & I come home. What a joy To see my wife & boy after a week. Feel exhausted plan a few days rest of course with some work each day. Am burning Mottos now. I certainly enjoy this work.

Spend rather quiet week I am having some terrific fights with reference to Temptation But GOD.

SUN July 8

Today Arnold & I start a weeks meetings in Los Alimitos — a small town with a great need. I speak on "The liberty werewith Christ hath made us Free".
about 20 out. no visible results; though hearts seemed touched.
John V. is playing
Chas Boggs of Penn drops in. Says he is go to study for ministry.

MON July 9

Meet S.S. Boys in A.M. plan a possible boys work. they seem to see the need. Talk to Pierce about — Of course he would like to see it linked with the church.

Meeting in Los Al. well attended Arn. K speaks on "Delivered from so great a death".

TUES July 10

Up Early — Shower — (Cold) Devotions = Today with Gods Help I expect to begin the MM. Duties (feeling the need for a definate plan) God will help me. (Wrote Gurney Brooklyn N.Y. need of MM. to be carried on.
Spoke at Los Alimitos on "Kept by the power of God".

Los Alimitos

WED July 11

Write Lester — Up rather late — Stan brings home — Gunn Woode-White sply for Burning Mottos — Make one 2x14 Phil 4:11. Surely enjoy this burning the Scripture — A new plan is to make Star one each of all I make for Samples & I'll keep me in wood.

Wed Class. Art & Mar — Clausing over with Les & Georgia — Great Int shown in study of Salvation.
Am Talking Time once again for a little on Beach with Bible.
Bruce can crawl slow forward or Aft. Sometimes when he starts he shoves it into the moony gear.

Bruce

THURS July 12

1. Today have victory in Tremendous battle.
2. Coates Back — Preaches Lu Alimitos Rom 8:37.
3. hears has a promised pardnership in Al.
4. Had a real need — the Lord sent See To us through Horton & Loss

Bruce & child Fear on pray that hill ns
Decease fear?

Preface

More than thirty years have passed since the last major book about Dawson Trotman was published. The book you are now holding includes excerpts from the largely unpublished writings of Trotman, including his personal journals, private correspondence, transcripts of conference sermons, and an unfinished book manuscript, *Faithful Men*, that was intended to be his *magnum opus* of disciple-making. It offers the reader, for the first time in decades, Dawson Trotman, in his own words.

In writing this book, we intend to spark interest in Trotman by bringing to light writings of historical significance and by reflecting on some of the ideas present in these writings and around which Daws built his ministry. Most of the "Daws quotes" in this book have never been published, and indeed most have never been read by anyone other than Dawson himself and the half-dozen people who have written about him over the past half-century. The authors hope that this book will lead, in part, to a wider publication of more of Trotman's original writings.

The first section of this book offers a brief essay on the life, thought, and legacy of Dawson Trotman. The authors hope that this section will serve as a refresher for people already familiar with Daws and as an introduction for people who do not know him well.

The second section of this book is comprised of fifty-two devotionals built around Scripture and excerpts from Daws' writings. The devotionals are grouped in accordance with the six elements of the Navigator Wheel. Trotman never elevated any one aspect of the Wheel over the others, and he never prioritized an order within or among these elements. Instead, he viewed them as interrelated and interdependent. While the authors have chosen to arrange the devotionals thematically, they sincerely pray that readers will move across topics as they feel led to do so, and that they will not feel bound to read the book sequentially. Within each topic, the devotionals are ordered chronologically so as to place Dawson in his historical context. The authors hope that this arrangement will give insight into the development of Trotman's theology. The authors also wish to make abundantly clear that although the devotionals offered in this book use excerpts from the writings of Dawson Trotman, the source and object of all of our devotion is our Savior and Lord Jesus Christ. We hope that Trotman's words might help point us toward the One who alone is worthy of all praise, honor, glory, and worship.

The third section of this book offers a selection of articles that Dawson Trotman created. The authors have included this section to give Trotman the chance to speak on his own terms, and to introduce people to his classic writings and illustrations. His more well-known works such as *The Need of the Hour* and *Born to Reproduce* are widely available. The articles that appear here are some gems that have seen less attention.

The authors have several goals in mind in writing this book. First, we pray that people will gain a clearer understanding of Dawson Trotman through a devotional presentation of some of his words. Second, we pray that people will be spurred to further research and writing about this fascinating and influential Christian man. Third, we pray that people will be challenged and encouraged to "get down to business" in growing as disciples and in multiplying disciples. Above all, we pray that people will draw closer to God as they read this book, and that everything we have written brings glory and honor to our Lord and Savior Jesus Christ.

THE NAVIGATORS

1. START.... APR. 1933 ...

2. CONCENTRATION OF EFFORT
   - 3 mon - SPENCER
   - 2 " HARRIS
   - 7 " { GOODRICK
          { DEDRICK

   II TIMOTHY 2:2 THEN

3. TOO RAPID GROWTH
   DIDN'T FOLLOW THRU.
   BUT........ { KEY MEN

4. PEARL HARBOR- { W. VA.

5. GROWTH
   STAFF
   FULLER

6. NAVIGATORS MISSION VISION
   ACTS 1:8 { BOTH
            { AND
   India 1927
   BIOLA 1929
   TYPE of CHALLENGE

7. NOW

WITH CONVICTION →

MOODY.	WESTMONT
WHEATON	UNIVERSITIES
BOB JONES	BIOLA
Phila.	
B.I. of P.A.	MISSIONAIRIES NOW!
EASTERN	

Hit HARD →

8. IN THIS GENERATION
   II COR 6

1. MULTIPLICATION
   The PICTURE

"LIFT UP THY VOICE!"

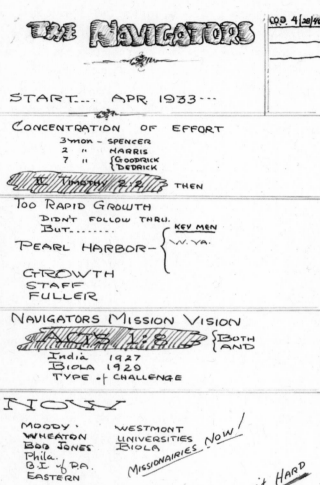
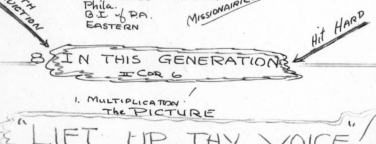

Dawson Trotman: Life and Legacy

Introduction

On January 3, 1945, Dawson Trotman wrote in his journal that he had met that day with a group of other Christian leaders to discuss plans for "the combining of forces . . . to accomplish the greatest possible amount in the shortest possible time in the most effective way." Few other phrases could express so succinctly the driving passion of the man who founded The Navigators and who is often called "the father of the modern discipleship movement." In just twenty-five years of public ministry, Trotman left a legacy that is only now, more than half a century after his death, being understood and appreciated. The enduring fruit of his ministry grew from his singular passion to accomplish more, to do it today, and to do it well. The root and ground of his ministry, however, was Christ.

Trotman founded his ministry in Christ, focused it on Christ, and dedicated it to the furtherance of the gospel of Christ. He firmly believed in biblical inerrancy, and he was convinced, beyond any doubt, of man's universal need for Christ. He never wavered in his commitment to the truth that all people everywhere deserve to hear the glorious good news of the gift of salvation offered by grace through faith in Christ. Trotman held himself bound by love and obedience to be fruitful, busy, and effective in sharing throughout the world the message that the gospel of Jesus Christ is the one and only way by which people may find the hope of the glory of God.

Few people today have ever heard Dawson Trotman's name, and fewer still know any of the pertinent details of his life, thought, and legacy. For people who wish to learn more about the life story of this key Christian leader, two excellent biographies are still in print: Betty Skinner's *Daws*, published through Zondervan in 1974 but now available through NavPress, and Robert Foster's *The Navigator*, published by NavPress in 1983. The following pages offer a brief biographical sketch of this larger-than-life, yet distinctly human, man.

Biography

Dawson Earle "Daws" Trotman was born on March 25, 1906, in Bisbee, Arizona. During the first ten years of his life his family moved several times, eventually settling in Lomita, California (a suburb of Los Angeles). Daws was a middle child with a sister, Mildred, who was three years older than him, and a brother, Rowland, who was five years younger. His father, Charles, had been baptized in the Anglican church as an infant but was a confirmed atheist as an adult. His mother, also named Mildred, became a follower of Aimee Semple McPherson, the charismatic leader of the Four Square Pentecostal denomination. Religious differences played a large role in their decision to divorce while Daws was in high school.

Despite his father's atheism and his mother's Pentecostalism, Daws joined Lomita Community Presbyterian Church, which he attended fairly regularly between the ages of fourteen and eighteen. Trotman's leadership qualities were evident during these years. He served as a leader of the church's Young People's Society for Christian Endeavor Club, which provided the primary opportunity for social life among young people of the town. In his senior year of high school he was the president of the student body, chairman of the student council, captain of the basketball team, editor of the school annual, and class valedictorian.

After high school, Daws stopped attending church. Despite his academic and social successes, he showed little interest in his future or in a career. In the era of Prohibition, he turned to smoking, dancing, gambling, and drinking as favorite activities. Over the next two years he had at least four significant brushes with the law related to public drunkenness. On the last occasion, he made a vow that if God would get him out of trouble, he would go back to church. Two days later, he returned to Lomita Community Presbyterian Church and attended a Sunday evening service, and three weeks later he professed a personal experience of salvation by grace through faith in Jesus Christ.

The story of his salvation offers a fascinating study in the power of God's Word, and formed the basis for one of his better-known messages, "Coming to Christ Through Scripture Memorization." When Daws first attended a meeting of the Christian Endeavor Club, he participated in a team Scripture memorization contest. Hoping only to impress a pretty young girl in the club, Daws spent the week memorizing ten verses of Scripture. When the next Sunday meeting rolled around, Daws was the only member of the club who could recite all ten verses from memory, and as a result his team won that week's contest. Pleased with his success, Daws memorized another ten verses during the second week, and his team won the contest again that week. During the third week, the truths of the Scripture he was memorizing began to convict his heart, and he was saved. Months later, Daws learned that his mother had been praying for his salvation and had shared her concerns with the women who supervised the Christian Endeavor Club. Not coincidentally, the Scriptures selected for the contest all related to sin, grace, and the saving work of Jesus Christ.

Daws' personal experience with the power of the Word of God in bringing him to salvation convinced him of the importance of the discipline of Scripture memorization. Through the years of his ministry, he grew even more convinced of the importance of Scripture memory work as a foundational element of everything related to Christian growth and maturity.

The years following Trotman's conversion can be placed within three ten-year periods: the Formative Period (1926–1936), the Sophistication Period (1936–1946), and the Production Period (1946–1956). (This historical periodization is described in detail in Doug Hankins' PhD dissertation, "Following Up: Dawson Trotman, The Navigators, and the

Beginnings of Discipleship in America, 1936–1956.") The first ten-year period (1926–1936) was a formational time for Dawson Trotman. While he was never ordained and did not experience anything like a specific calling to ministry, Daws nonetheless came to understand that he had a role to play in God's kingdom. To use one of his own favorite expressions, he simply "got down to business," reading, studying, and memorizing Scripture, and teaching as many people as possible how to do the same.

His first ministry opportunity as a new Christian was teaching a young boys' Sunday school class at Lomita Community Presbyterian Church. This assignment lasted until 1931 when a disagreement over the nature of the Bible resulted in a church split, with Trotman and the pro-inerrancy group forming a new Bible church in Redondo Beach. Trotman briefly served as the pastor of this newly formed church, after which he enrolled in the Bible Institute of Los Angeles (BIOLA) and Los Angeles Baptist Theological Seminary for two years.

During his seminary years, Trotman became involved with an evangelistic group known as the Minute Men, which consisted of men who were "armed and instantly ready to do spiritual battle for the Lord." These BIOLA students functioned as highly disciplined gospel teams that were skilled in the areas of personal spiritual disciplines, soul-winning ability, and expertise in establishing boys clubs. In addition to his Minute Men activities, Trotman also participated in a group called the Fisherman's Club, an evangelistic program for young men built around Scripture memorization and apologetics.

In 1933, a mutual friend from BIOLA referred a sailor named Les Spencer to Daws for spiritual advice. During the half-dozen years following his conversion, Daws had been memorizing Scripture steadily at the rate of more than a verse a day. He had been actively involved in the daily practice of intentional evangelism, and he had determined at a very early point in his Christian walk never to be caught without a Bible answer to any question or to any objection to faith in Christ. Spencer quite simply had never met anyone who had the command of Scripture that Daws demonstrated, and he wanted what Daws had. When Daws felt certain that Spencer had a sincere desire to "get down to business," he began investing much of his time in discipling this young man.

After some time had passed, Spencer wanted to bring one of his sailor friends to Daws for discipling, but Daws refused to do so. Instead, he insisted that Spencer disciple this friend himself. The Navigator ministry began out of this simple event. In the years between 1936 and 1946 (the Production Period), Daws developed methods and structures for reproducing himself in younger Christians, initially through a general approach to discipleship, and eventually through a formal ministry organization called The Navigators. As Daws later wrote in a 1956 magazine article for the *Park Street Spire*,

> We tried [in the early years of the Minute Men ministry] to get decisions. And we got them. Yet, as I took inventory and checked back, I found a year later that those decisions that had been made hadn't been followed through. I reached the conclusion in talking to many people that perhaps challenge might be considered 2%, getting the decision 5%, and getting that decision carried out 95% [*sic*]. Out of that discovery The Navigators was born.

With the arrival of Les Spencer and several other servicemen, Daws began pouring himself into the spiritual growth of a small group of Navy men, whom he in turn held accountable for doing the same thing with other men. His home served as a general meeting place where sailors could come for spiritual teaching and encouragement, and some men came to live in the home whenever duties would allow. This practice of designating a Navigator Home became the standard model for the expansion of the Navigator ministry over the next several years.

In the years prior to World War II, The Navigators discipled hundreds of Navy men based at the busy port of Long Beach. As the war approached, most of these men were moved with the Pacific Fleet

to Pearl Harbor and the ministry of discipleship multiplication continued to grow. After the bombing of Pearl Harbor and the entry of the
United States into the war, the Navigator ministry spread all over the
globe, first through the Navy and the Marines, and eventually through
the Army as well.

By the end of World War II, Navigator-trained men numbered in
the thousands. As these soldiers returned home and took up new lives in
businesses, schools, and churches, the Navigator ministry adapted and
began to view these areas as new mission fields. This period of expansion
(1946–1956) marked the third and final period of Trotman's life, which
was a time of great productivity in The Navigators organization. The late
1940s saw The Navigators emerge nationwide as the leaders in "follow-
up" ministry. Through his personal contacts with, and widening
influence among, evangelical leaders, Daws eventually worked at the
highest levels with most of the major evangelical Christian organizations
of 1940s' and 1950s' America.

In 1952, The Navigators was unexpectedly presented with an
opportunity to partner with Billy Graham to purchase Glen Eyrie, a
seven-hundred-acre ranch located in Colorado Springs, Colorado. After
Graham pulled out of the deal, he turned the option to buy the property
over to The Navigators. Friends from all over the world contributed
generously, and the property was purchased six weeks later. The
Navigators relocated from California to Colorado at the end of 1953,
and its ministry expanded to include the hosting of conferences, retreats,
and training seminars.

Just three years later, on June 16, 1956, Dawson Trotman drowned
at Schroon Lake in the Adirondack Mountains region of New York. The
East Coast Navigator staff had been assembled there for a spiritual retreat
and conference. On a trip across the lake, Daws and a young girl were
thrown overboard when their powerboat hit some rough water. Aware
that the young girl could not swim, he held her afloat until the boat was
able to circle back and pick them up. Just as the girl was rescued, Daws
sank out of sight and drowned.

Theology

Trotman held broadly conservative and evangelical convictions. As noted, he attended seminary for a few semesters, but he leaned most heavily on the sufficiency of Scripture in contrast to any teachings or doctrines of specific churches or denominations. He was a firm believer in the person and work of the Holy Spirit in bringing illumination to people who diligently applied themselves to the study of God's Word, but he also was leery of the emotional excesses of churches that focused too narrowly on looking for specific signs of the working of the Holy Spirit. He was willing to partner with any person and any group that was sound on what he considered to be the essential matters of the Christian faith (doctrines dealing directly with God, man, sin, and salvation) and was unwilling to sever relationships with people who differed on what he considered to be secondary matters (doctrines related to the administration of the sacraments, structures of church polity, detailed system of eschatology, and so on).

In the specific area of ecclesiology, Daws had a high theoretical agreement with the concept of "the church" as the body of Christ, but he had a low view of the expression of that body in specific local congregations. While in most matters Daws developed his theological positions from his study of Scripture, he formed his views on church membership largely from his personal negative experiences with specific congregations. Doctrinal divisions related to the modernist/fundamentalist controversy tore apart the Lomita Community Presbyterian Church in which Daws had come to faith in Christ. The church plant he helped start saw minimal growth despite sound theology. As the Navigator movement grew among the sailors in San Diego, he witnessed churches that refused to welcome the "raw" new believers. He grieved over the small number of Christians who were actively engaged in witnessing their faith, and he saw little evidence of spiritual growth and maturity among the overwhelming majority of the Christians of his day. In all of these things, he blamed the leaders of local churches, who he felt were more interested in maintaining their jobs and their status than in maturing their flocks.

A terse journal entry from Sunday, February 3, 1946, reveals the general low regard with which Daws viewed most churches: "[Spoke] at a small church in _____. Usual deadness. Hit hard with a challenge. Several younger men really responded." Stated most simply, Daws saw "the need of the hour" as too overwhelming and the time too short for him to be bothered with trying to reform the thinking and practices of churches or their leaders. He was too impatient for such a task, and he was pessimistic about the potential for effecting change at this level. Instead, he viewed local churches as fishing grounds for prospects and as mission fields for his maturing disciples. He expected his men to be "at church" somewhere every Sunday, but he never expected them to feel or act like they were actually members of any local church.

Methodology

While Daws was conservative in his theology, he was anything but traditional in his methodology. He was not open to new ideas about the authority of Scripture or the exclusivity of salvation by grace through faith in Christ, but he was always open to new tools and new methods for making Christ known and in maturing believers in their walk with Christ. With respect to methodology, it is fair to say that he was innovative, contextual, nontraditional, and above all, pragmatic. If a new tool or a new resource seemed to be helping men "get down to business," he used it until he found or developed a better tool or resource.

His pragmatism with respect to methodology was largely the result of his personal experience. In his testimony, he told the story of giving a ride to a hitchhiker one day and launching into a presentation of the gospel, only to discover that he had met this same man more than a year earlier. On that previous occasion, this young man had made a profession of faith in Christ, but then he had been abandoned and now he showed no visible evidence of his faith in Christ making any difference in his life. This encounter convicted Daws. Along with his commitment to getting "down to business" in Scripture memory and doing the personal work of daily evangelism, he now added the responsibility to follow up with every new believer and do everything possible to "reproduce reproducers." Trotman coined this term to describe the process of growing new Christians into mature believers who would then lead new Christians to grow into mature believers. Trotman drew biblical support for this principle from 2 Timothy 2:2, which he called simply "the 2:2 principle." The constantly evolving methodology of Daws' ministry was the result of his determination to learn how to achieve and balance all these tasks most effectively.

Through the years, Trotman developed several theological illustrations for specific aspects of the Navigator work. Four of his tools that remain in use in The Navigators today are the Bridge to Life, the Word Hand, the Prayer Hand, and the Wheel.

The Bridge to Life illustration is one of the best-known and most widely used evangelistic presentations, yet few people today realize that it was introduced in America by The Navigators. Daws learned that

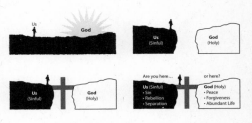

Navigators working in the Far East were using this gospel presentation with great effectiveness. The Bridge to Life clearly presents the gospel and lays the foundation for discipleship ministry, because only people who are in a relationship of saving faith with Jesus can be "discipled" to maturity in their faith. Daws recognized the simplicity and effectiveness of this presentation, and he made it a standard part of Navigator training. According to Daws, all disciples should actively share their faith, which means that all new disciples should learn this as a matter of first priority.

The Word Hand illustration uses the five fingers of the hand to illustrate five essential elements of comprehensive Bible study. Moving across the fingers from "pinkie to thumb," the first finger represents hearing the Word, the second reading the Word, the third studying and

applying the Word, the fourth memorizing the Word, and the last meditating on the Word. As Daws would say, it takes all five fingers being used together for anyone to be able to grasp and hold onto the truths of Scripture with a firm, full grip. Just as Daws had determined never to be caught without a "Bible answer" for any question or any objection to Christ, he also determined that new believers must learn as a matter of first priority how to go to God's Word for every answer and every issue.

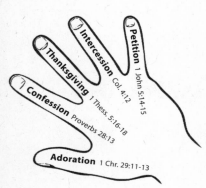

The Prayer Hand illustration also uses the five fingers to illustrate five essential aspects of a robust prayer life. In this tool, the five fingers represent adoration (voicing our worship of God), confession (agreeing with God about personal sin), thanksgiving (recognizing God for what He has done), intercession (praying for others), and petition (asking God to meet personal needs). Daws knew that prayer was the vital connection between believers and God. Witnessing without prayer leads only to human effort without the power to achieve supernatural results. Bible study without prayer produces only knowledge without the wisdom to understand and apply it. Daily life without prayer creates only ineffective legalism and a life without peace, joy, or fellowship. According to Daws, new believers also need instruction and encouragement in prayer as a matter of first priority.

Without a doubt, the single most recognizable symbol of The Navigators is its most foundational tool, the Wheel illustration. In his early ministry years, Daws sought to develop a suitable illustration for the Christian life. In his three-legged stool analogy, the "legs" of prayer, the Word, and witnessing (each with their own illustrations and tools, as previously noted) all supported the Christian life. However, Daws quickly discarded the stool analogy, because he did not like the symbolism of the Christian "sitting down on the job." Because he was already working with Navy men, Daws chose to use the Captain's Wheel as his main illustration.

He made "living the Christian life" the rim of the wheel, but soon realized that three spokes were not enough. He included in this developing symbol a fourth spoke, fellowship, for the mentoring relationships within which disciples are made. In the final version, he placed Christ at the center of the Wheel, and the symbol was complete. Trotman's personal journals contain several ink drawings of the Wheel in its early stages of development.

Due to the substantial influence of The Navigators, the Wheel model of discipleship spread throughout the evangelical churches of the world. Any system of discipleship that incorporates intentional aspects of direct instruction using these elements likely traces its root to Trotman and The Navigators. The fifty-two devotionals that form the body of this book are organized around this distinctively "Navigator" symbol and model.

Significance and Legacy of Trotman's Ministry

It may be impossible to fully ascertain the extent of Trotman's impact on Western evangelical Christianity. However, his legacy can be studied, and in some degree measured, in light of his personal influence with the individual Christian leaders of his day and through the continued vitality of The Navigators as an organization despite the early death of its founder and leader.

His journals recount details of his personal relationships with scores of influential evangelical leaders of the mid-twentieth century. The list of people with whom Daws worked regularly and closely includes Charles Fuller, Cameron Townsend, Jack Wyrtzen, C. Stacey Woods, Jim Rayburn, Bob Evans, Thomas Talbott, Lewis B. Smedes, J. Edwin Orr, and Billy Graham. Through his connections with key Christian leaders, Daws exerted a shaping influence on the organizations they founded and led, and thereby on the multitudes of people they reached.

Even a partial listing of the organizations with which Daws partnered is astonishing. On a significant level, Trotman personally assisted in key aspects of the founding, development, or ministry of the Billy Graham Evangelical Association, Wycliffe Bible Translators, Fuller Theological Seminary, Young Life, Youth for Christ, Campus Crusade for Christ, InterVarsity Christian Fellowship, Mission Aviation Fellowship, China Inland Mission, Overseas Missionary Fellowship, Africa Inland Mission, the Evangelical Foreign Mission Association, Operation Mobilization, and Overseas Crusades.

Through these organizations, and through The Navigators themselves, Trotman's theology and methodology of disciple-making became part of the status quo of evangelical thought and practice across most of the evangelical Christian world. While many of the relationships that Daws formed were significant for the development of the contemporary Christian landscape, two in particular seem worthy of special attention.

The relationship between Dawson Trotman and William Cameron Townsend (the founder of Wycliffe Bible Translators) influenced both organizations. Through his involvement with Townsend, Daws became a member of Wycliffe's board of directors in 1942. A few years later, Trotman sent his secretary, Vivian Fusby, and her new husband, Ken Watters, to work for Wycliffe, where they remained for the rest of their careers in the ministry. More than five hundred Navigators eventually accepted his challenge to become Wycliffe missionaries following World War II. Daws personally oversaw the recruitment and training of most of Wycliffe's missionaries throughout the late 1940s and early 1950s. Wherever Wycliffe missionaries went across the globe after World War II, they took Trotman's discipleship theology and methodology with them.

Trotman's influence on the Billy Graham Evangelical Association is also noteworthy. Daws met Graham on a visit to Wheaton College in 1941. Graham later recounted this experience: "I hadn't been with him five minutes until he was challenging my life and probing to the depths of my life," and on a second visit the next year Daws directly challenged Graham on the subject of Scripture memorization. In 1950, Daws was asked to design, lead, and implement a comprehensive program for the follow-up of new believers from the Graham crusades. In the foreword to a transcript of Trotman's message *The Need of the Hour*, Graham later wrote, "I think Dawson Trotman touched more lives than any man I have ever known. Thousands of people of many races and languages and cultures have been influenced by this great man." In the foreword to Bob Foster's biography of Trotman, Graham also wrote, "The very extensive follow-up system we now have, which [is] the most intensive and extensive in the history of so-called 'mass evangelism,' actually came from Dawson Trotman's heart and mind."

Finally, through the ongoing vitality of Navigator structures and resources Trotman's legacy extends from his own lifetime down to the present. The written materials he left behind, though few in number, are still in publication. In addition, vast numbers of Navigator-trained men and women continue to serve in virtually every area of the evangelical church world.

The Navigators thrives as an organization committed to Trotman's legacy of disciple-making. Founded in 1975, NavPress publishes books, Bible studies, and other discipleship resources. The Glen Eyrie Conference Center hosts more than one hundred retreats, seminars, training events, and conferences each year. As of the last staff census taken in 2008, The Navigators had 4,647 staff members of 70 nationalities working in 108 countries.

Many of Trotman's evangelism and discipleship methods and materials are still used more than fifty years after his death. Since 1976 (the first year in which circulation records were established) NavPress has sold more than 365,000 copies of Trotman's Topical Memory System. The booklet *Born to Reproduce*, which lays out Trotman's concept of spiritual multiplication, has been translated into nine foreign languages and has had sales in excess of 400,000 copies. The pamphlet form of Trotman's "new disciple" Bible study course, *Beginning with Christ*, has had more than 1,600,000 copies distributed worldwide in fifteen languages. The Billy Graham Evangelistic Association still publishes and uses the booklet *Thirty Discipleship Exercises: The Pathway to Christian Maturity*, written in 1957 by one of Daws' key leaders, Charlie Riggs, from materials and methods created by Daws himself.

Conclusions

Dawson Trotman was one of the most influential and significant Christian leaders of the twentieth century. Over the course of a twenty-five year public ministry, he personally mentored hundreds (and indirectly discipled tens of thousands) of men and women who became leaders of the American evangelical Christian mainstream, and he helped shape the direction of dozens of schools, seminaries, missionary groups, and parachurch organizations.

Trotman's singular focus on "follow-up" brought a new element to the mass-evangelism strategies of American evangelicalism. His methodologies of evangelism follow-up, one-to-one discipleship training, Scripture memorization, and spiritual multiplication now form the basis for much that is considered to be conventional wisdom with respect to the disciple-making strategies of the contemporary church, even as his person and legacy fade into obscurity.

While Daws exerted significant influence during his life, his enduring legacy is evident in the multiplied thousands of Christian workers and leaders who were trained, either directly or indirectly, according to his methods and principles. During the war years, Daws began the practice of sending out some form of regular communication newsletter to all of The Navigators scattered around the world. The name and format of this communication piece changed several times, but for many years it was called the *NavLog*. In June 1950, Daws wrote in *NavLog* #41, "We are not out to raise monuments to man's creeds and accomplishments, but we are looking to GOD to raise up living stones—monuments to His grace—yielded young men and women whose eyes are singled to His glory." The thousands of "yielded young men and women whose eyes are singled to His glory," who have served in ministry over the past seventy-five years and who continue to be won to faith in Christ, brought to maturity in Christ, and sent out in service for Christ, are Trotman's most significant and enduring living legacy.

In light of all this, however, it is important to remember that Daws was very human, with feet of clay, and with some glaring personal weaknesses. His associates regularly noted that he could be demanding, overbearing, insensitive, driven, aggressive, and lacking in patience. He often insisted upon extremes of performance that even he could not always sustain. In a journal entry of March 3, 1932, he noted that the Minute Men had agreed to follow a list of seven daily spiritual tasks. On August 28, that list was expanded to nine, and by September 4 it was increased again to twelve. In typical Daws fashion, he developed forms and charts to track the specifics of performance for each person, and he graded and made extensive comments on each piece of homework the sailors turned in. Eventually, the whole system was replaced with something simpler.

On a personal note, his family at times felt neglected. Many "preacher's kids" feel that everyone gets attention except them, but Daws took this a step further with any number of sailors likely to be staying at the house all day, overnight, through the weekend, and often even longer. Within The Navigators organization there were many times when friends were hurt or angered and when differences of opinion on matters of leadership and direction ended with people leaving under strained circumstances. Some of the ruptures of fellowship resulted in a permanent loss of unity and friendship. But through it all, and despite the more glaring deficiencies in the organization's leader (who was, to be fair, doing pioneer work, often learning by trial and error), God worked in unimagined ways. The fledgling group of sailors with their civilian mentor seemed to be just the kind of weak thing that God delights to use to shame the strong.

More than fifty-five years after the death of its founder, The Navigators is still struggling to come to grips as an organization with its relationship with Daws. He is larger than life in many respects, and yet he was very human in reality. Revered and respected on the one hand for his proven accomplishments and legacy, he must also be recognized for his faults and weaknesses. The founder of any significant organization will appear to be legendary and mythic to a generation of members who never knew him, but it was never Daws' intention that The Navigators stay anchored to its own past. In the pages that follow, we have the first opportunity in nearly thirty years to listen to Daws in his own words, to read what he had to say about his own walk with Christ and his advice on growing in the faith. May we heed God's command to "test all things, holding fast to what is good," and may we be spurred on by the passion and vision of Dawson Trotman to get "down to business" in the Lord's work, until Christ returns or calls us home.

Christ the Center

DEC.   CONSIDE HIM

I Remember
II Tim 2:1-8 Jesus Christ

The
WORD PROMISES
VICTORY
COMPLETE
{
JUDE 24
I COR 10:13
II COR 2:14
Eph 6:16
II Thes 3:3
}

The Victorious Life is the Exception Rather Than The Rule

. THE SECRET (People Look for A)
                          Secret

ONLY ONE - The LORD JESUS CHRIST | II Cor 1:10 |
                                      | Phil 4:13 |

REMEMBER JESUS CHRIST.

Remember THE ALAMO !! 1836

            1941 Disinity then
    The Jap Sneak ATTACK.

REMEMBER PEARL HARBOR !! (Demo.
                          Repub.
                          Cap.
                          Laber

I TEMPTATION *Consider Him*
   HE WAS
   HE CONQUERED
   HE Sustains

II FOR OTHERS
    Phil 2:3, 4 (This Mind
    Rom 15:3
    NIGHT Before Death .
       He Comforts.
    John 13;14 — ETC .

III The LOST
     Mat 9: 36-38
     WEPT
     PRAYED   and Before
     LIVED WITH THEM
     DIED—
     LUKE 2:52 .

1

In Life or Death, Christ Is All

Yes, and I will rejoice, for I know that through your prayers and the help of the Spirit of Jesus Christ this will turn out for my deliverance, as it is my eager expectation and hope that I will not be at all ashamed, but that with full courage now as always Christ will be honored in my body, whether by life or by death. For to me to live is Christ, and to die is gain.

PHILIPPIANS 1:18-21

Journal Entry, January 11, 1937

"For the past weeks God has been dealing with me. The more I see of my life the more I touch the Hem of HIS garment, the more I realize that no good thing can happen until the Lord deals with me. I am aware of the fact that the Lord is working something in my heart that is more than ordinary. Oh that HIS name might be glorified through my life whether by life or death."

When Paul wrote his epistle to the saints at Philippi he was in prison and thus unable to help them directly, but he was heavily burdened for them and for the many other congregations of saints he had helped to form across the Roman world. He was concerned about his own trial and, indeed, about his own life. He was concerned about issues of doctrine, practice, and personal conduct that were only beginning to emerge as former Jews and former Gentiles in dozens of different cultural settings began to grasp some of the implications of identifying themselves as followers of "the Way" of Jesus Christ. In addition, he had a personal investment in the spiritual growth of many young men, some of whom had already begun to drift away from the truth, either by returning to religious legalism or by falling victim to emerging heresies. And yet, in the midst of all his care and concern, Paul never lost sight of the reality that he was expendable, that the advance of God's kingdom would continue even if he should die, and that no matter what he felt he had "personally" accomplished, he had done everything only through and for Christ.

By early 1937, the Navigator ministry was fully launched among the Navy men in San Diego, with significant works in progress on the *West Virginia, Texas, Maryland, New Mexico, Mississippi, Pennsylvania,* and *California,* and many other ships. Daws was still searching for better tools for discipling the men, for better methods of forming and sustaining Bible study groups, and for better systems in maintaining accountability and control of everything that was taking place. At home his son, Bruce, had just turned three and his daughter, Ruth, was nine months old. His wife, Lila, had recently had some health issues, and another family was living in their home (the first official Navigator Home had not yet been purchased, but this aspect of the ministry was already taking shape in practice). In addition to all of this, Daws was still active with the Minute Men and at BIOLA, and he was always busy enlisting the support of churches and individual Christians throughout the region. Only a handful of men in the history of modern Christianity have experienced firsthand being at the center of such a mighty movement of God. Daws was aware that God was doing something "more than ordinary," and he could have easily believed that this somehow made him indispensable to the growth and continuation of the work.

In the excerpt from Daws' journal quoted above, we see echoes of several passages of Scripture. When Daws wrote of "seeing more of his life" in direct relation to God, he may well have been thinking of Isaiah 6:1-8. In talking about "touching the hem of HIS garment," Daws clearly had in mind the story found in Matthew 9:20-22, Mark 5:25-34, and Luke 8:43-48. Just as clearly, in his desire to glorify Christ only and always, whether by life or death, Daws was quoting fragments of Philippians 1:20-21.

In light of all of these observations, two simple truths are evident in this journal entry. First, the more the Word of God is poured into a person, the more it flows out of a person. Second, when the Word of God dwells richly in someone over a long period of time, the natural result is a life that is centered around Christ, that sees itself rightly related to Christ, and that seeks ultimately to glorify Christ. Daws was willing to spend and be spent for Christ. He was willing to live and continue to work for Christ, or die and allow God to continue this great work without him if that was what would be best in God's sight. Like John the Baptist (see John 3:30), he was willing to be diminished, if by that Christ might be magnified.

Lord, help me to remain humble no matter what ministry You may give me. Help me to seek to always keep You at the center of all that I do, even if it brings me to the point of recognizing that Your work might be better accomplished without me. For as long as You give me kingdom ministry to perform and kingdom works to do, may I remember that I bring glory to Your name only by Your will and Your power. May You always be the center of all I am and of all I do, and when it is time for me to place my work in other hands, may I do so with confidence and joy because I have always known that those other hands were Yours all along.

(KEN)

2

The Way, the Truth, the Life

Jesus answered, "I am the way and the truth and the life. No one comes to the Father except through me."

JOHN 14:6 (NIV)

S.T.S. Bible Study (ca. 1941)

"The Lord Jesus Christ is my Saviour. HE is the true WAY to God. HE is the true and living WAY to God. What a wonderful way, and I'm not trying to find it. I'm on it. My heart is thrilled! I must take some others with me."

In 1940 Dawson Trotman created a new Bible Study method called "S.T.S.," which stood for Study to Shew Thyself Approved unto God, based on 2 Timothy 2:15. Trotman and The Navigators filled out worksheets using the acrostic STUDY:

- S—Summary
- T—Title
- U—Uplift, Spiritual
- D—Difficulties, Personal
- Y—Your Key Verse

In late 1940–1941, the team studied the gospel of John. Dawson filled out the S.T.S. study just like everyone else and recorded his thoughts on the passages that he read. In his meditations on John 14:6, he rejoiced over Christ as the way, the truth, and the life.

In John's account of the Last Supper, Christ tells His disciples that He is going away to prepare a place for them and will come again to take them there. "And you know the way to where I am going" (verse 4). Thomas reminds Jesus that they don't even know where He is going, much less the way to get there. Christ responds, "I am the way, and the truth, and the life. No one comes to the Father except through me" (verse 6).

In his personal study of this passage, Daws rejoiced over the revelation of the way to the Father. He didn't have to search out different religions or philosophies to find the path to God. Instead, this true way had been revealed through the person and work of Jesus Christ.

Trotman desired to take others with him on this journey. He would spend his entire ministry devoting himself to the spread of the gospel and to helping believers grow in their faith as they trod along the path of the Christian life. Daws closed his meditation on John 14 by stating, "It is my desire to be used of HIM to train men to live for HIM, and who will work out with a willingness to lay down their lives for HIM. I know He will grant this desire of my heart. He is partially granting it now."

Lord, please reveal the True and Living Way to the others around me, and grant that we may grow in our love for You as we travel this way together.

(SUSAN)

OBEDIENCE

MISTAKEN Idea O.T. only. Mat 5:17   I say unto you.
I Sam 15:- Rev. Brown

OBED.- really discovering and
keeping the   WILL OF GOD.

Heb 5:8.

Greatest of   SON
Virtue   SERVANTS
               SOLDIERS

COMMANDMENTS OF CHRIST
            173
Mat 5,6,7
Gospels.
John 13 - 16
Acts - Solid One
Rom - 12+4, 15 16 same
I Cor -

Jas 1:22
Mat 7:24 - 29   WISE
                 MAN

THE SECRET OF MIGHT MEN

TRUST & OBEY ← ABRAM.----- Heb 11
MOSES
JOSHUA
DANIEL
DAVID

Deut 11:26
Blessing
Curse.

JOHN 14:   PROMISE   Josh 1:8

THE HAND.

MEMORY.
  1. Direct Order.
  2. MEANS

DAY OFF.
  1. Thus Saith the Lord.
     a- Unsaved. Mat 7
     B- Saved ----
     c- Satan.
  2. Every Decision
  3. Basis for all Study
  4.

Finding the will of God.

Scripture Shed light on Song

Obedience Is the True Measure of Love

When they had finished breakfast, Jesus said to Simon Peter, "Simon, son of John, do you love me more than these?" He said to him, "Yes, Lord; you know that I love you." He said to him, "Feed my lambs." He said to him a second time, "Simon, son of John, do you love me?" He said to him, "Yes, Lord; you know that I love you." He said to him, "Tend my sheep." He said to him the third time, "Simon, son of John, do you love me?" Peter was grieved because he said to him the third time, "Do you love me?" and he said to him, "Lord, you know everything; you know that I love you." Jesus said to him, "Feed my sheep."

JOHN 21:15-17

S.T.S. Bible Study (ca. 1941)

"Feed my lambs; feed my sheep." Christ had already called them to be fishers of men and had promised that if they would follow, HE would take care of that end of it. Now HE was assigning another work, a work ever so important, that of taking care of those who had been won. These passages have always been a great challenge and blessing to me with regards to the work the LORD has called me to in spending so many hours with those who have been won. I believe I can see that the greatest investment of time with regards to winning the greatest number to CHRIST is made through this method, for then those I lead to HIM and lead on with HIM become soul winners. Hence, the work can be considered by multiples rather than by additions."

Most commentaries on the gospel of John devote considerable space to the three verses that relate the final encounter between Jesus and Peter. In three of the best-known commentaries, much discussion focuses on the specific wording found in Jesus' questions and Peter's answers. It is carefully noted in each that two distinct words for "love" are used in the Greek text. One word, *agape* (Greek, αγαπάς), emphasizes the self-sacrificial aspect of love. The other word, *phileo* (Greek, φιλώ), emphasizes the brotherly affection aspect of love. The author of each commentary reviews the many theories regarding whether or not the use of these words is of particular significance. It is also carefully noted in each commentary that Jesus questions Peter three times, and the authors all review the many theories regarding whether or not this repetition of questioning is related to Peter's threefold denial of Christ.

Each commentary also notes that Jesus responds to Peter's answers with variations of the phrase, "feed my sheep." One author observes that feeding sheep has "pastoral implications" and that Peter later became associated with pastoral leadership of the early church. Other than that, most commentaries are silent about these words of Jesus.

Daws was on-to something important here in identifying the phrases "feed my lambs" and "feed my sheep" as central to the interpretation of this passage of Scripture. Yes, there is value in studying every word used in Scripture, and yes, Peter clearly needed to be restored, but both of these are secondary issues in this text.

Three times Jesus asks Peter a question, and three times he responds to Peter's answers with a phrase for which the preceding question appears to be merely a setup. It seems clear that Jesus is providing Himself with the opportunity to say, and then repeat, and then repeat again *one thing* that He *really wants* Peter to understand. "Do you love me? Feed my sheep!" The point is not that Jesus doubts Peter's love or even the kind of love Peter professes. Even Peter "gets" this point, saying, "Lord, you already know all things." Rather, the point is that Jesus wants to say, and say again, and then say once again, "Feed my sheep!" until He is sure that Peter "gets it."

In early 1941, Daws was finally beginning to "get it" also. He had been working for enough years with enough men to realize that he could not personally evangelize every sailor in the Pacific Fleet. Near the end of his life, John would write, "For this is the love of God, that we keep his commandments" (1 John 5:3). Peter was commanded three times to show his love for Jesus by feeding the sheep of Jesus. Daws built his ministry around making sure that the sheep got fed, knew how to feed themselves, and knew how to teach others to do likewise.

Lord God, as children who love You, our hearts yearn to obey You. We acknowledge that You are worthy of our full obedience, and we know that You delight in our obedience, and yet we must confess that we are too often satisfied with partial obedience. We feel ourselves to be well fed, and we assume that others feel likewise. We lead people to the place where food is available, only to leave them to feed on their own. Three times, Lord, You command us to be active in feeding Your sheep! As we love You, may we obey You in this, and in all things.

(KEN)

4

God's Protecting Hand

Though I walk in the midst of trouble, you preserve my life; you
stretch out your hand against the wrath of my enemies, and your
right hand delivers me.

PSALM 138:7

Journal Entry, January 1, 1942

"Morena Downing arrived home, an evacuee from Honolulu. She tells
us of the mighty way God is working in the lives of men who know
Him and of the difference between those who have a hope in God
and those who have none . . . Cole is missing. Cole has been the
weakling all these years on the *California*. In contrast God's
protecting hand on a yielded man, Parker, two days before the
disaster was transferred to Palmyra. . . . He was really yielded
and committed his life to the Lord. Urged by the fellows before
the war to get out of being transferred to Palmyra he said, 'No,
I'm committing my life into His hands.'"

Throughout the mid- to late 1930s, The Navigators were a small
group of men and women working primarily in the Los Angeles area
and the Navy. Young sailors gathered aboard ships such as the U.S.S.
West Virginia to study Scripture with other Christians. Amid the
economic and social upheaval of the Great Depression, American
spiritual life was at a low tide and many of the Navigator servicemen

wrote home about the spiritual opposition they encountered aboard their ships.

The Japanese attack on Pearl Harbor on December 7, 1941, changed everything for The Navigators, and for the nation. That weekend, Navigator Jim Downing had liberty from his ship, U.S.S. *West Virginia*, which was anchored with the U.S. Pacific Fleet in Pearl Harbor. On Saturday Jim and his wife, Morena, went to their usual Bible study at the Navigator Home in Honolulu, and as the hour grew late they decided to stay the night. On Sunday morning Morena cooked breakfast for her husband and the six other Navigator sailors in the home. Suddenly the ground below them began vibrating and a series of explosions rocked the house. As the sky filled with black smoke, they heard on the radio, "The island of Oahu is under enemy attack."

Downing and his shipmates rushed back to Pearl Harbor and found utter devastation. Jim slid down the gun barrel of the U.S.S. *Tennessee* to reach the oil-covered deck of the *West Virginia*. He manned a fire hose and kept the ammunition lockers aboard the ship from exploding. One hundred feet away flames from the U.S.S. *Arizona* leaped skyward, and across the harbor the U.S.S. *Oklahoma* foundered belly-up. The U.S.S. *California* sank into the harbor. Navigator Francis Eugene Cole died aboard the *California*, along with ninety-seven of his shipmates. The man who Dawson Trotman had once thought the weakling of his ship died with a Bible in his hand.

Parker escaped the attack, however, when he was transferred to the *Palmyra* only two days before. His former shipmates had tried to convince him to stay with them, but he decided to submit to the Lord's direction, and thus missed the attack by forty-eight hours.

In the days following the attack, Morena Downing gave blood at the local clinic and prepared for evacuation. She left the island on a transport ship on Christmas Day, not knowing if she would ever see her husband, Jim, again. Upon her arrival in Los Angeles, she told the Navigator staff stories about sailors who had previously mocked the gospel but were now eagerly attending Jim's Bible studies held in bomb shelters. Dawson wrote, "Significant in the general run of things as far as human beings are concerned is the oft repeated story that during the time of danger, hearts were opened." Downing and his friends had dedicated their lives to memorizing Scripture and to spreading the gospel, and they were thus able to effectively minister to the souls ravaged during the attack.

There are no easy answers why Francis Cole perished in the attack while his fellow Navigators Parker, Downing, and Ken Watters were spared, but Dawson Trotman attributed the salvation of the latter three to God's protection on lives fully yielded to Him. Sometimes the Lord works through ordinary, mundane events to preserve us from the Enemy's attack. As they had done so many times before, Downing, Watters, and several other Navigators had chosen to spend their Saturday night of liberty studying Scripture at the Nav Home, and were thus not aboard their ships the next fateful morning. There was nothing unusual about the Navy's transferring a sailor from one ship to another, but the Lord used these orders to spare Parker's life.

Whether you face a very real physical enemy as the Navigators did on December 7, 1941, or are wrestling with the deadly Enemy of your soul, be mindful to follow the Lord's leading even in small ways that may seem ordinary to you. Attending your weekly Bible study may not necessarily save your life in the midst of a disaster as it did Jim Downing, but digging into the Scripture will help preserve your heart and prepare you to share Christ with the perishing. Commit your life to following Christ and trust that He protects and defends His beloved. "The Lord knows how to rescue the godly from trials" (2 Peter 2:9).

For your name's sake, O LORD, preserve my life! In your righteousness bring my soul out of trouble (Psalm 143:11)!

(SUSAN)

5

Christ,
My Righteousness

For Christ is the end of the law for righteousness to everyone who believes.

ROMANS 10:4

AlphAmegA Bible Study, Romans 10 (December 2, 1942)

"V. 1-5, Christ the Holy One is my righteousness now because I believe no more of this vain attempt to appear righteous by any of my deeds. V. 17, This is what I long for—I have all the Word, hence I can have all the faith through receiving, hearing, reading and studying the Word."

In 1942, Dawson Trotman created the Bible Study Worksheet "AlphAmegA" for his Dunamis Club. The AlphAmegA study was divided into three main portions, all of which began with *A*:

- Approach: in which the scholar was supposed to begin the study with prayer and a preliminary reading of the passage.
- Apprehension: a summary of the passage and thoughts on the key passage and key questions.
- Application: thoughts on the personal and practical.

This is Dawson Trotman's personal application on Romans 10:1-5,17.

Growing up in the Lomita Community Presbyterian Church, Daws tried all sorts of things to justify himself apart from the work of Christ. He became a leader in Christian Endeavor. He was his high school valedictorian, student body president, and captained the basketball team. The only thing that this overachiever couldn't manage to obtain on his own was true righteousness. After realizing that these good deeds were merely a veneer that hid a multitude of sin, he fell into a rebellious lifestyle of heavy drinking and general mischief.

One day, on his way to work at a lumberyard, John 1:12-13 flashed into his mind and he gave his life to Christ. He gained "the righteousness of God through faith in Jesus Christ for all who believe" (Romans 3:22). Christ is the fulfillment of the law that Dawson could never have hoped to keep on his own.

Oh, Christian overachiever, are you trying to appear righteous by all of your good deeds? Rest in the fact that Christ is your righteousness. As you read and study the Word, do so not to appear righteous before your fellow church members or your friends who haven't yet turned to Christ. Instead, receive and meditate on the Word out of gratitude for Christ's finished work.

Lord, please forgive me of all my vain attempts to appear righteous by my own deeds. Thank You for imparting righteousness to me through Christ; Christ is my righteousness now.

(SUSAN)

6

Spending Time in God's Word

So faith comes from hearing, and hearing through the word of Christ.

ROMANS 10:17

Personal Bible Studies in the Christian Life (ca. 1942)

"So from the start it is our desire to direct you to spend time daily in the Word of GOD and to urge you to approach it with open mind and responsive heart.

"The most important thing in a new Christian's life is to learn the great truths of GOD's Word and how to appropriate them. The Bible not only claims to be the Word of God and is the means by which we are saved, but actually plays a very important part throughout our Christian life. For example: Romans 10.17 says that we receive faith through the Word; Psalm 119.105 shows that we are directed by means of the Word.

"NOTE: While personal study of GOD's Word is paramount in the life of the victorious Christian, it should by no means be considered a substitute for regular fellowship with others in His Church. 'Not forsaking the assembling of ourselves together, as the manner of some is; but exhorting one another: and so much the more, as ye see the day approaching' (Heb. 10.25 [kjv]). It is GOD's plan for His children to be instructed by men chosen of Him. 'And I will give you pastors according to Mine heart, which shall feed you with knowledge and understanding' (Jeremiah 3.15 [kjv]; also see Ephesians 4.11,12)."

In this introduction to *Personal Bible Studies in the Christian Life*, Dawson Trotman outlined the importance of studying the Word, letting it work in your life, and having regular fellowship with other believers.

During the early days in the Navigator Home, Daws made sure that serious study of the Word occurred in the context of fellowship. In addition to meditating on Scripture with his friends, Daws made a point to have fun with them. He and his men played volleyball in the front yard, croquet on the lawn, and enjoyed Lila's delicious dinners.

In *Life Together*, Dietrich Bonheoffer talked about the power of preaching the gospel to one another. Our own hearts deceive us and are prone to wander unless we are in the fold with other believers. Another Christian can remind us of Christ's marvelous saving work on the Cross. We can process together, pray together, and lead one another to the throne of grace. A Christian who grows in the context of community and fellowship with other believers is a sweet gift from the Lord. It cheers us and gives us a picture of what the future kingdom of heaven will be like. Exhort one another, read Scripture together, and let the Word sink down deep into your responsive heart.

Lord, please help me spend time in the Word daily. Please open my mind and heart to receive what You have for me. Also, please lead me into fellowship with other believers who will encourage me to know and love You better.

(SUSAN)

7

The Purpose of The Navigators Was Each "Navigator," Not "The Navigators"

So then you are no longer strangers and aliens, but you are fellow citizens with the saints and members of the household of God, built on the foundation of the apostles and prophets, Christ Jesus himself being the cornerstone, in whom the whole structure, being joined together, grows into a holy temple in the Lord. In him you also are being built together into a dwelling place for God by the Spirit.

EPHESIANS 2:19-22

NavLog #41, June 1950

"We are not out to raise monuments to man's creeds and accomplishments, but we are looking to GOD to raise up living stones—monuments to His grace—yielded young men and women whose eyes are singled to His glory."

One of the serious and harmful side effects of three decades of the church growth movement is that it has encouraged too many leaders to focus too much of their time, energy, and resources on building great churches rather than on building great Christians. In our efforts to grow our ministries, many of us have forgotten that great churches are not the same thing as large churches. Some churches are both and some are neither, but all churches should strive firstly to be great and secondarily to be large. After all, the temple of God is no longer associated with a physical structure. The dwelling place for God by the Spirit is the gathered body of Christ, each member joined together and built together.

By 1950, The Navigators had grown into one of the most influential parachurch Christian organizations in history. Navigators numbering in the tens of thousands were serving in churches, on mission fields, in Christian organizations, and in secular vocations. Daws was personally working directly with the Billy Graham Evangelistic Association, Wycliffe Bible Translators, Mission Aviation Fellowship, China Inland Mission, Fuller Theological Seminary, Young Life, Youth for Christ, Campus Crusade for Christ, InterVarsity Christian Fellowship, and a host of other Christian organizations. In just three more years, The Navigators would purchase the Glen Eyrie property and establish a permanent home for their global ministry. Along the way, Daws regularly reminded himself that it had never been his intention to create a "great" organization. Rather, the greatness of The Navigators as a group was the natural result of their ongoing passion to focus primarily on building great Christians.

Once Daws realized that follow-up was the key to Christian growth and maturity, doing that one task with greatness of purpose and greatness of effectiveness was his overriding concern. When he wrote this *NavLog* article, he was not blind to the actual accomplishments of The Navigators, nor was he blind to the danger of loving too much the greatness of the organization he had helped to create. As The Navigators continued to grow, he wanted to make sure that they continued to do so by growing great Christians rather than great institutions.

This *NavLog* message had a clear point and a simple word of caution. The purpose of The Navigators was always found in each individual Navigator, in each separate person who was raised up with his "eyes singled to His glory." The seductive allure of relying upon the greatness of The Navigators as a corporate entity was always present for Daws, but he knew that the world already had enough monuments to man's accomplishments. Daws was accused at times of focusing too much on numbers and reports, but as this message to all of "the gang" makes clear, he wanted to remind everyone (including himself) that the purpose of The Navigators was to be used of God "to raise up living stones—monuments to His grace—yielded young men and women whose eyes [were] singled to His glory." Numbers were always a secondary concern.

Lord God, the allure of worldly greatness and the temptation to build and maintain monuments to our own accomplishments are ever with us. May we always look to You and be reminded of our primary purpose as people who are called out of the world yet remain in it, as people who are being joined and built together into a dwelling place for You by Your Spirit. May we be used of You to build the only monument that endures: people who worship You now and forever.

(KEN)

8

God Leads the Way in Evangelism

See, I have set the land before you. Go in and take possession of the land that the LORD swore to your fathers, to Abraham, to Isaac, and to Jacob, to give to them and to their offspring after them. . . . See, the LORD your God has set the land before you. Go up, take possession, as the LORD, the God of your fathers, has told you. Do not fear or be dismayed. . . . The LORD your God who goes before you will himself fight for you, just as he did for you in Egypt before your eyes.

DEUTERONOMY 1:8,21,30

Possessing the Promises, Speech Given July 17, 1951

"NEARLY EVERYBODY THAT I TALK TO about memory of Scripture says, 'Well, I just have a poor memory.' THEY START OUT THAT WAY. THEY'VE GOT AN EXCUSE. 'I don't have time. I wish I could.' They have a little excuse of some kind. Gang, as I look back over my own life and ministry I can see that there were many little places where decisions were made and a step was made that didn't seem so big to me then, but I can see that if it wasn't taken then it would have just cut out everything that God has wanted to do in my life since. And I would point out to you that once the Lord first promises you what is yours, you will come to find out what it is. Learn these precious promises. Learn the things that are yours in Christ. Learn the commandments of moving forward. Learn Deuteronomy 1:8 and learn Deuteronomy 1:21 and 1:30 and learn these challenging verses that drive you ahead. And then after you learn them, and God gives you a chance, step out. Do the difficult thing as you make your steps."

It was said of Dawson Trotman that he was a simple man with a simple plan. This statement was both true and false at the same time. Daws was a complex man, driven and yet friendly, contemplative and yet basic, serious and yet a jokester. And his plan may have been simple in scope and in the component makeup, but the plan was personally challenging and intimidating to many Christian leaders in his day. Thus, Trotman could describe his plan as involving "little" decisions that resulted in "big" outcomes.

In 1951 Trotman was in the midst of developing and training personnel for the Billy Graham Crusade Follow-Up Team. The content of this speech was nothing novel for Trotman; he had likely given this same challenge multiple times before in individual and group settings. But this particular speech had the weight of Trotman's amassed influence behind it and was likely being given to a new generation of leaders who knew Trotman only as the father of the modern discipleship movement.

The steps were simple: First, locate God's promises in Scripture. Trotman knew that God does what He already said He is going to do. Daws did not recommend that people search long and hard about God's specific will for their lives (although he was certainly sensitive to crises of faith). Rather, Daws suggested that people find out what God was already doing and then jump on board.

Second, this proposal was accomplished through careful biblical study and memorization of God's Word. Once someone located God's promises, they were instructed to memorize it and hide it in their hearts. This act transformed Scripture from a reference book to a spiritual weapon. Now, Trotman would say, one is prepared for battle.

Third, God will give you a chance—so go do something with it. Trotman was not big on having the circumstances just right. He encouraged Christians to move as soon as there was an opportunity. For a swimmer who is getting ready to swim laps, rather than waiting until the water is at the perfect temperature and the waves have settled, Trotman would suggest that the swimmer jump in as soon as the water is available for swimming. This was not a license to be foolish or reckless in the way someone went about sharing the gospel. It was instead meant to be an encouragement that we do not need to be intimidated by the task at hand, because God has invited us to join Him in sharing the gospel.

God, thank You for leading in gospel sharing. Thank You for equipping us with Your Word. Thank You for preparing the way for us. And, thank You for promising us an inheritance in the gospel. We will join You in doing something for the kingdom.

(DOUG)

FOLLOW THRU

THE WORD DEMANDS ---

They Profess But in Works they deny.

EPH 2:8,9 --- 10
Tit 3:5 ---- 8
I COR 3:11 ---- 12-15
John 14:6 ----- 15,21,23 etc.

Faith alone that saves but the faith that saves is never alone

JOHN 1:12 --- COL 2:6,7

DID THE APOSTLES BELIEVE IN FOLLOW THRU.   PETER James, JOHN

JOHN ---   JOHN 3:16   5:24   NOTE
   III John 4.   18   6:47.   Chapters
                    36   14, 15

                                    Rev. also II Tm. see
                                    overcomes — I Jn 5:4,5
PETER -----   I Pet 1:18   LIVING HOPE   note.
                  1:23   1:5
                  2:24   1:3,4. =   1:14
                  3:18   1:22
                                           2:9,1)
                                           2:21

{ II Pet 1st chap }

PAUL -----   Note
         I Thes 1:9

PROOFS.

1. His STAY -- Acts 18+20

2. His Preaching -- II Tim 2:2.   II Tim 4:1,

3. His Example Acts 20^{16:31,32}.

4. God shut him up. The Epistles.

9

Follow Through on That Decision

Therefore, if anyone is in Christ, he is a new creation. The old has passed away; behold, the new has come.

2 CORINTHIANS 5:17

"Follow Through on That Decision," in *Youth for Christ,* September 1954

"First, you need to know clearly what happened when you made that transaction with Jesus Christ. Second, realize what it will mean in your life. Then, make up your mind to learn the secret that will make you a winner. . . . Just what did happen when you said yes to Him? If you once for all realized that God 'made Him (Jesus Christ) to be sin for us, Who knew no sin, that we might be made the righteousness of God in Him' (2 Cor. 5:21 [KJV]) and received Him into your life, here's what took place: You became a son of God—you were born right into His family, just as surely as you were born into your own. Christ Himself took up residence in you and the Holy Spirit became your own personal Guide and Teacher throughout life. Everywhere you go, He goes. You have suddenly inherited tremendous riches and privileges that would take a long time to count. What difference will there be in your life then? There should be plenty. You'll never be the same as before."

In an article for *Youth for Christ* magazine in 1954, Dawson Trotman outlined what happens when we place our faith in Christ and how to grow in this relationship. In John 14:6 Jesus told His disciples, "I am the way, and the truth, and the life. No one comes to the Father except through me." In Antioch, the apostle Paul preached, "Let it be known to you therefore, brothers, that through this man forgiveness of sins is proclaimed to you, and by him everyone who believes is freed from everything from which you could not be freed by the law of Moses" (Acts 13:38-39). After Paul and Silas miraculously escaped from their prison chains, their jailer asked, "What must I do to be saved?" Paul replied, "Believe in the Lord Jesus, and you will be saved, you and your household" (Acts 16:30-31).

Once you believe that Jesus is the Lamb of God who has taken away the sin of the world, several marvelous things happen. You become a member of the family of God, a son or daughter of the Most High. As a child of the King, you can expect both chastening and blessing, fellowship with your heavenly Father, and direct access to the throne of grace. The Holy Spirit indwells you and becomes your comforter and guide who will teach you all things and bring back to your remembrance what Christ has done for you.

Dawson Trotman knew the importance of helping new followers of Christ understand this transformation. He wanted new Christians to begin reading the Bible, to memorize Scripture, and to apply it to their lives. While evangelists like Billy Graham focused on leading people to place their faith in Christ, Trotman focused on helping them grow in their faith. The Navigators partnered with the Graham team to follow up with the people who indicated that they had made decisions for Christ. Navigator staff members stayed behind after the Graham crusades to meet with people one-on-one, encouraging them to memorize Scripture and teaching them how to pray.

Have you made a decision to follow Christ? Move ahead in this direction. Learn what God is saying to you through His Word and fellowship with Him in prayer. Let what He has revealed to you through

Scripture and the Holy Spirit sink down deep into your life and transform you. God is making you into a new creation—and you'll never be the same as before.

Jesus, I believe that You are sent from the Father to take away the sin of the world. Thank You that while You were perfect and without sin, that You became sin for me, that I might gain the righteousness of God. Please spend the rest of my life teaching me what this means for me, and use me to share this good news with others.

(SUSAN)

10

Exalt the Lord, Jesus Christ

Oh, the depth of the riches and wisdom and knowledge of God! How unsearchable are his judgments and how inscrutable his ways! "For who has known the mind of the Lord, or who has been his counselor?" "Or who has given a gift to him that he might be repaid?" For from him and through him and to him are all things. To him be glory forever. Amen. I appeal to you therefore, brothers, by the mercies of God, to present your bodies as a living sacrifice, holy and acceptable to God, which is your spiritual worship.

ROMANS 11:33–12:1

Our Wonderful Lord, L.A. Area Men's Conference (April 8, 1956)

"I just wanta read these verses [Romans 11:33–12:1] as we stop and gaze upon the One Whom we serve. One of the reasons I love the Young Life work . . . is that my, you can hardly go to a meeting where they don't exalt the Lord Jesus. I love Campus Crusade work for that same reason. And Inter-Varsity, and I wanta tell you that I praise the Lord for these great works. We have the president of Fuller Seminary coming to our Staff Conference this year—Dr. Carnell. And as I talked about it yesterday, I said, we would see Jesus, and we could ask, how would Dr. Carnell be about presenting the Lord to us, just give us messages every day about the Lord . . . I praise the Lord for Fuller. And for every other group. I praise the Lord for every group that is exalting the name of the Lord Jesus."

It is no secret that The Navigators worked closely with other key evangelical organizations throughout the forties and fifties. Trotman was a personal friend and mentor to Bill Bright of Campus Crusade for Christ, C. Stacey Woods of InterVarsity Christian Fellowship, and Jim Rayburn of Young Life. In this speech, the wise and seasoned Trotman draws upon his relationships with these leaders as an example to the Navigator men about just what should be the mark of any Christian organization — the exaltation of Jesus Christ.

The goal of this message was to exalt Jesus Christ as Lord by understanding the reason for Christ's worthiness. Trotman looked to Paul's words in Romans 11:33-36 as the context for his command in Romans 12:1. In verse 36 Paul said that Jesus Christ is the origin of all things, the sustainer of all things, and the goal of all things. In other words, Jesus Christ is the reason for *everything* in existence. By contrast, consider some forms of Hindu cosmology that conceive of three gods, one who creates, one who sustains, and one who destroys. This polytheistic worldview necessitates worship of three beings for three different reasons. Each form of worship is incomplete without the other forms.

But Paul was saying that Jesus Christ is the origin, means, and end of all of creation and thus Christian worship is complete in Him. This was a profound point that Paul was making. And it was a rallying point for Trotman and the Navigator men present at the conference.

Trotman could say of his ministry, as Bill Bright, C. Stacey Woods, and Jim Rayburn could of their respective ministries, that the goal and desire of The Navigators was that in all things Jesus would be the focal point. Trotman challenged the men to consider the exaltation of the name of Jesus Christ the most important task in life.

God, along with the apostle Paul, we cry out to You, "For from him and through him and to him are all things. To him be glory forever. Amen" (Romans 11:36).

(DOUG)

The Obedient
Christian in
Action

11

Daws Never Lost Focus

Not that I have already obtained this or am already perfect, but I press on to make it my own, because Christ Jesus has made me his own. Brothers, I do not consider that I have made it my own. But one thing I do: forgetting what lies behind and straining forward to what lies ahead, I press on toward the goal for the prize of the upward call of God in Christ Jesus.

PHILIPPIANS 3:12-14

Journal Entry, November 15, 1929

"Definite memory of Scripture—definite continual reading of Scripture—builds the prayer life, which growing makes the working vital Christian [*sic*], and indeed fruitful."

Journal Entry, January 1955

"The time has come where some definite business (1) with referent to looking up men is concerned must be done (2) memory must be resumed (3) prayer must be renewed in a real sense."

Daws began keeping a regular journal in August 1929, but aside from some very sporadic entries in 1953 and 1955, he had pretty much stopped this practice for most of the last decade of his life. The two quotes above represent one of the earliest and one of the latest references from his journals. Despite the twenty-five-year separation of these two quotes (covering the entirety of the ministry of The Navigators), one cannot help but be struck by the unity of thought expressed here. In particular, these passages clearly display three key elements of the Navigator method.

The first is personal follow-up. Daws' early journal entries contain dozens upon dozens of references to "looking up" men. As The Navigators grew into a worldwide organization and the demands on Daws' time grew ever greater, he never lost his passion for personally connecting with individuals.

The second is Scripture memory. At the very beginning of his ministry, Daws focused in a singular way on Scripture memory, mastering first one verse a day, then two verses a day, and eventually as many as three verses a day. As he neared the end of his ministry years, he was still consumed with holding himself accountable with regard to Scripture memorization. Think about this for just a moment. If Daws had memorized only one verse a day through the twenty-five years between these two entries, he would have memorized more verses than are found in the entire New Testament. If he had memorized two verses a day over this period of time, he could have memorized the New Testament plus Genesis, Exodus, Leviticus, Numbers, Deuteronomy, and almost all of Psalms.

The third is prayer. At no point in his life does Daws appear to have been content with the state of his prayer life, and throughout his journals he revealed that he was regularly convicted of his neglect of prayer, and of his lack of effectiveness in prayer.

The apostle Paul, nearing the end of his ministry life, reminded "the saints in Christ Jesus who are at Philippi, with the overseers and deacons" (Philippians 1:1) to focus on what still remained to be done. Despite all that he had accomplished, including being used of God to actually write much of what would become the New Testament, he never felt that he had "arrived" as a follower of Christ. Daws apparently never felt that he had arrived with respect to Scripture memory, prayer, and witnessing. He never lost his focus on the primary principles of personal gospel work, personal Scripture work, and personal spiritual work.

Lord God, keep us ever mindful that our personal focus should always be on sharing the gospel, on growing in our knowledge and understanding of Your Word, and on staying close to You in prayer. May we never become distracted from these daily practices, no matter how busy or how burdened or how "big" we may become. May we, at the end of our lives, still burn with the passion of our first love for You, and may it be enriched by years of faithfulness and perseverance in service to the singular pursuit of bringing glory to You.

(KEN)

12

Examples of Faith

Therefore, since we are surrounded by so great a cloud of witnesses, let us also lay aside every weight, and sin which clings so closely, and let us run with endurance the race that is set before us, looking to Jesus, the founder and perfecter of our faith, who for the joy that was set before him endured the cross, despising the shame, and is seated at the right hand of the throne of God.

HEBREWS 12:1-2

Journal Entry, January 1, 1937

"The Word is indeed precious and the Living Word—Christ—becomes more precious to me. Reading the Life of Spurgeon by Day has been a very great blessing and strengthening to me in these last few days. How my heart is thrilled as I see a man who wholly yielded to my Saviour and brought such Honor to His Glorious Name."

In late 1936 and early 1937 Dawson Trotman began reading about the famous preachers of the nineteenth century including Charles Spurgeon and D. L. Moody. Dawson found the lives and words of these preachers a great encouragement in his own Christian life and challenged himself to live up to their godly example.

Charles Haddon Spurgeon was one of the most influential preachers in England and earned the nickname the "Prince of Preachers." Born June 19, 1834, Spurgeon received Christ in 1850. He began preaching shortly thereafter. In April 1854 at age nineteen he answered a call to pastor London's New Park Street Chapel, where he would remain for the rest of his career. His congregation grew to upward of ten thousand and crowds regularly gathered to hear him preach. Stenographers recorded his sermons, which were sold for a penny per copy. These sermons and Spurgeon's other voluminous writings were later compiled into several daily devotionals. In addition to his work in evangelism, Spurgeon also founded a preacher's college, the Stockwell Orphanage, and wrote and compiled hymns. He died in January 1892.

Forty-five years later, Dawson Trotman spent New Year's Day 1937 reading Richard Day's *The Shadow of the Broad Brim: The Life Story of Charles Haddon Spurgeon*. In his journal, he reported that he found the experiences a blessing and encouragement. A few days later, he started reading *Bush Aglow* about the life of D. L. Moody, the evangelist from Chicago. Dawson remarked, "I see so many things happening in this man's life that are like events of my own life that I am strengthened as I realize that others whom God has used have had the same heart struggles as I have. Paul in Romans 7 speaks of this, but it seems to bring it so near to me to read concerning the life of one of His servants who lived such a short time ago."

Dawson Trotman had many of the same heart struggles that you do, and you may find many things happening in Dawson's life that resonate with your own experience. The God that Dawson Trotman, Charles Spurgeon, and D. L. Moody served is the same God who reigns today and forever. It is good to remember how He has worked through the lives of His servants to bring honor and glory to His name. These men struggled with many of the same problems that you do: busyness, financial trouble, depression, and heartache. The same God who comforted Spurgeon during his bouts of depression and who provided for the Trotmans on days when they had no money for food is the same God who cares for you.

Lord, thank You for the work that You have done in Your servants of the past. Thank You for the women and men who fully yielded themselves to You and who brought honor and glory to Your name. Please continue to provide examples of saints whose lives were like my own and who triumphed in Christ.

(SUSAN)

13

Work While It Is Today

We must work the works of him who sent me while it is day; night is coming, when no one can work. As long as I am in the world, I am the light of the world.

JOHN 9:4-5

S.T.S. Bible Study (ca. late 1940/early 1941)

"This verse constantly challenges me to get going, to get down to business, not to waste time, not to procrastinate. It is bad enough now. There is sin and disease and war and trouble through-out the world, but it is still according to this verse 'day' and 'night cometh when' I can do nothing about these things. May God strengthen me to accomplish His will while there is yet time."

In his personal devotions Dawson Trotman studied the gospel of John throughout late 1940 and early 1941. During this time there certainly was trouble throughout the world, as Europe and Asia had already plunged into the terrors of a second world war. Hitler had begun his march across Europe, and the Japanese army occupied China. Trouble did, indeed, consume the world in late 1940–1941.

Trouble was coming for The Navigators too, and Daws anticipated what life would be like for his sailors if the United States entered the war.

At the end of 1941, he would find out. On December 7, 1941, the Japanese attack on Pearl Harbor drew the United States into the global conflict. The Navigators lost shipfitter Francis Cole aboard the U.S.S. *California* that day. Those who survived the attack, such as Jim Downing, would immediately enter into battle in the Pacific. During the time Daws was meditating on John 9, however, he and The Navigators were enjoying a few last golden months of peace. They had the chance to fellowship freely, to witness, and to conduct spiritual business without immediate peril hanging over them.

In John 9, Christ warned His disciples to walk in the light while they still have the light. For a few more months, the disciples could learn as much as possible from their Master while He was still on earth. Christ predicted His death and the physical and spiritual darkness that would cover the earth. Very soon His followers would be hunted and persecuted, Jerusalem would fall to the Romans, and the early church would be forced underground. For the time being, though, His followers could walk in the light while they still had the light.

With so many global crises all around us today, with sin so prevalent in the world, we must remember that we are to get busy. In the United States, we still have the freedom to witness to our loved ones and to study the Word freely. Only God knows for sure when another night will fall, so we must take advantage of these freedoms while we can. Let us therefore get going, stop wasting time, and stop procrastinating. There is much work to do, and now is the time to do it.

Father, please help us to get down to Your business and to stop wasting time. Please strengthen us to accomplish Your will while there is still time.

(SUSAN)

14

Clinging to Christ

I have said all these things to you to keep you from falling away. They will put you out of the synagogues. Indeed, the hour is coming when whoever kills you will think he is offering service to God. And they will do these things because they have not known the Father, nor me. But I have said these things to you, that when their hour comes you may remember that I told them to you.

JOHN 16:1-4

S.T.S. Bible Study (ca. late 1940/early 1941)

"If we are clinging to his words, the words of men and the actions of men cannot upset or offend us."

In John 16, Christ warned His disciples that trouble was looming. Members of their own synagogues would kick them out of the congregation. Their own religious leaders and neighbors would soon be after blood. Christ warned that this would happen because the troublemakers do not know the Father or believe in Christ. Jesus let His disciples know what was about to take place in order to encourage them to cling to the truth.

You may not be in mortal peril as the disciples were after Christ's death and resurrection, but you surely will encounter people who will cause you pain, even in the church. These hurts may come through bitter comments, neglect, abuse, or pride. Sometimes the people who wound you may even think they are doing so in God's service.

Dawson Trotman wrote, "The surest way to prepare against being offended by these things which shall occur in our lives is to know HIS Word, to know what HE has said regarding these things." Has someone made you feel unloved or unwanted? God says, "You are precious in my eyes, and honored, and I love you" (Isaiah 43:4). Has someone lied about you? The psalmist asked, "Vindicate me, O God, and defend my cause against an ungodly people, from the deceitful and unjust man deliver me!" (Psalm 43:1). Has someone excluded you because you follow Christ? Jesus told His followers, "Blessed are you when people hate you and when they exclude you and revile you and spurn your name as evil, on account of the Son of Man! Rejoice in that day, and leap for joy, for behold, your reward is great in heaven" (Luke 6:22-23). For every unjust wound against you, the truth of God's love and grace is waiting for you in His Word.

Lord, please guide and comfort me with Your Word and Spirit so that the actions of others do not wound or offend. Thank You for speaking words of truth and love to me!

(SUSAN)

<u>ULTIMATE GOAL</u>⎫
GLORIFY GOD. ⎬ SPOKE OF SOME
              ⎭

LEAD UP TO FRUIT -- as mean of multiplying

WHAT KIND OF MEN <u>WILL</u>
      Yielded men

- The life
- Praise
- Prayer.
- Suffering
- unity.

and

———— ⋲⋲⋲ FRUIT ⋑⋑⋑ ————

FRUIT
MORE FRUIT
MUCH   " --- ABIDETH ----

CONTRAST JUDE 12

        Lets Look AT THIS WORD
             FRUIT.

*A MAN
A YIELDED MAN
AN ABIDING MAN*

HUSBANDMAN - WAITETH ---- Jas 3:18

FRUIT OF THE SPIRIT ----- Gal 5² 22, 23
     - BRAKE DOWN =

FRUIT OF LIPS --- THANKS --- Heb 13:15

FRUIT MAY ABOUND - *GIFTS! Represents Time Involved* Phil 4:17
                    Rom 15: 27, 28

FRUIT AMONG YOU ----- Phil 1:22-24
            GROWTH-- Rom 1:13

*DANGEROUS TERRITORY
WE FEAR NOT*

FRUIT - TREE OF LIFE --- PROV 11:30
     WINNETH SOULS ---- ISA 61:3

*GENESIS THE KEY
BE FRUITFUL AND MULTIPLY*

      THE NEED. ———→

15

The Result of Obedience to God's Word Is a Blessed Life

Blessed is the man who walks not in the counsel of the wicked; nor stands in the way of sinners, nor sits in the seat of scoffers; but his delight is in the law of the LORD, and on his law he meditates day and night. He is like a tree planted by streams of water that yields its fruit in its season, and its leaf does not wither. In all that he does, he prospers. The wicked are not so, but are like chaff that the wind drives away. Therefore the wicked will not stand in the judgment, nor sinners in the congregation of the righteous; for the LORD knows the way of the righteous, but the way of the wicked will perish.

PSALM 1

AlphAmegA Bible Study (ca. 1942)

"Vs. 2, Especially challenges me to meditate in the Word day and night, literally to have it on the tables of my heart that I can meditate and thus produce fruit for my GOD.

"As a result of being obedient to GOD'S law, to live in the
Word day and night, I will be one of GOD'S blessed men (happy)
& will always be nourished within and thus be healthy outwardly
before the world."

Dawson Trotman was certainly a product of his time period. The early
twentieth century in America was a time when science reigned, when
enlightenment thought dominated culture, and when mechanistic
approaches produced results. Daws was famous for his adage, "Emotion
is no substitute for action. But action is no substitute for production. We
want productivity not activity." He was someone who expected God to
work in history and positioned his life accordingly. If a Christian was not
seeing results, Trotman had a clear-cut diagnostic checklist for discovering what was lacking—Psalm 1.

As his journal entries reveal, Trotman believed that the "blessed
life" was the normal and supernatural result of a disciplined effort of
"meditating" and obeying the Word of God. Trotman defined the
"blessed life" with three words: "happy," "nourished," and "healthy."
Trotman's vision of discipline was not a militaristic one, despite his military surroundings and naval officer constituency. Trotman was a militant man, for sure, but his militant approach was fueled by a satisfying
and happy life. His drive was for God and the joy set before Him, not
in maintaining a rigorous schedule.

Trotman was also someone who viewed the Bible as spiritual nourishment and was consistent to feed on Scripture throughout each day. The
Bible was not viewed as a cherry on top of the sundae or as the vitamins
for his main diet of culture or worldliness. Trotman's main meal was the
Bible, and he consumed it regularly. Finally, Trotman strove to be healthy
in his expectations of the Christian life. A better word for Trotman's
outlook might be "balanced." Trotman certainly had his share of ups and
downs. But it was not all ups, and it was not all downs. It was healthy and
balanced.

The happy, nourished, and healthy life that Trotman had in mind was strikingly different from what is generally proposed in the "prosperity gospel" preached throughout the globe today. Trotman found his prosperity in the Bible, in meditating on it, in studying it, in memorizing it, and in sharing it with others. The church could stand to adjust its posture in light of the model and example of Dawson Trotman.

God, thank You for the good food of Your Word. Nourish us with it. Make us healthy from it. And satisfy us with overflowing joy through it. Most of all, teach us to share the good food with others.

(DOUG)

16

Taking Time for People

Now an angel of the Lord said to Philip, "Rise and go toward the south to the road that goes down from Jerusalem to Gaza." This is a desert place. And he rose and went. And there was an Ethiopian, a eunuch, a court official of Candace, queen of the Ethiopians, who was in charge of all her treasure. He had come to Jerusalem to worship and was returning, seated in his chariot, and he was reading the prophet Isaiah. And the Spirit said to Philip, "Go over and join this chariot."

ACTS 8:26–29

Journal Entry, January 6, 1945

"A lot to do today. As usual, when I am most rushed, it falls to my lot to make the decisions whether or not I will spend time with individuals. Could easily have left a fellow for [ ] to take care of, but the LORD led me and I am sure that business was done that will count for eternity in this man's life in the 30 minutes we had together.

"This happened again at night when, with lots of reasons before me that I should not talk to [ ] about family affairs, yet I had a covenant made with the LORD that this would be done. It was. Again I see the LORD's hand. It will play an important part in all future relationships."

By January 1945, Dawson Trotman did have a lot to do. That month he busied himself making preparations for a trip to the Navigator Home in Honolulu. He planned on speaking with Ken Watters about "Reproducing Reproducers," a newly termed concept that would influence The Navigators' ministry into the future. He had just recently returned home to California after meetings with Young Life and Wycliffe. And, three days before Christmas, Lila had given birth to their son Charles Earle. With a newborn added to the already-busy household, Daws certainly did have a lot to do.

In the midst of this chaotic season, Daws could have easily become task-driven at the expense of his family and friends. On January 6 he had to make a conscious effort to spend time with a Navigator sailor instead of getting more work done. Daws obeyed the prompting of the Spirit to talk with the man and was later grateful that he did. During the same busy night, he also made a conscious effort to sit down and talk with someone about family affairs. He could have easily postponed these matters after a long day of ministry, but he chose to spend time with this family member in order to strengthen his relationships at home.

Who are the individuals in your life with whom you need to spend time? Are you neglecting your spouse or children because you have so much to do in your ministry? Are you ignoring your friends because you need to finish that school assignment or work project? Doing your work well and in a timely manner is a great virtue, but this work must not come at the expense of another human being. Your friend's soul is eternal—your project is not. When forced to choose between the two, pick the one that lasts.

Lord, please govern my time and help me to know when to spend time with the individuals You've placed in my life. Please help me manage my tasks so there is room for people.

(SUSAN)

17

The Obligation of Disciple-Making

To equip the saints for the work of ministry, for building up the body of Christ, until we all attain to the unity of the faith and of the knowledge of the Son of God, to mature manhood, to the measure of the stature of the fullness of Christ, so that we may no longer be children.

EPHESIANS 4:12-14

V-Mail #16, August 14, 1944

"As Children of GOD, what is our chief business? There is no doubt that yielded CHRISTians and those who know the Word of GOD will agree whole-heartedly that our chief aim in life is to glorify GOD and that our business is to fulfill the desires of HIS heart. How can we glorify HIM? . . . Only those who really know and follow CHRIST are in a position to bring . . . glory to HIS Name. Have we any right then to lead a man to make a decision for CHRIST and leave him there? Our job is only begun. Our obligation now begins."

Infants are incapable of bringing glory to their parents. They may be adorable, good-natured, and even amusing, but it is simply impossible for them to do anything worthy of glory. Infants cannot do anything heroic, astounding, or creative, because, after all, they are merely infants. When they begin to learn to walk, to eat solid food, and to talk, their parents may, and should, feel justifiably proud and happy, but there is nothing "glorious" in these actions. Children are generally expected to master these skills at certain ages as a normal part of healthy development.

Just as it is the natural role and responsibility of parents to educate, equip, and encourage their infants as they move through the common stages of early childhood development, the "spiritual parents" (or leaders) of the body of Christ bear the responsibility for helping new believers grow from spiritual infancy to mature adulthood so that they will "no longer be children." While God is always glorified in the "new birth" of a believer, spiritual infants bring no further glory to God by remaining helpless infants who have not yet learned how to walk (live the Christian life), eat solid food (read, study, and absorb the Word of God for themselves), and talk (share the gospel and speak of the things of Christ with other people).

By August 1944, Daws had come to the point of the full development and expression of his thought and method with respect to the process of building up mature, fully equipped followers of Christ through the work of The Navigators. In this excerpt from a letter sent to Navigators worldwide, he observes that only those people who are truly mature in Christ (who know *and follow* Christ), are capable of living in such a way that their lives and actions bring glory to God. Just as people can physically do glorious things only when they are involved in situations and events where glorious actions are possible, spiritual infants must be "spiritually positioned" to be able to glorify God.

Daws knew that this process would not happen by itself, but that Christ had given mature, gifted believers to His body who were to be used of God in bringing people to the point where they could begin to truly bring glory to Him. Moving people from spiritual infancy to spiritual maturity, he stated, is not an optional activity for the mature Christian. Spiritual "newborns" are expected, and in fact even commanded, to move from infancy through childhood to maturity. It is our job, and in fact it is our obligation, to educate, equip, and encourage them in this growth. Through our participation in this process, we position new believers in a way that makes it possible for them to bring ever-increasing glory to God.

Lord God, Your Word tells us that You have placed us within Your body and given us spiritual gifting for a singular purpose: that we might be used of You to equip other saints as they grow from spiritual infancy to spiritual maturity. Keep us mindful, Lord, that it is both our privilege and our responsibility to do so. May we bring glory to You, Father, both in ourselves and in the people we disciple who grow to be able to bring even greater glory to Your Name.

(KEN)

18

Making Mature Disciples Takes Time, Effort, and Skill

To [His saints] God chose to make known how great among the Gentiles are the riches of the glory of this mystery, which is Christ in you, the hope of glory. Him we proclaim, warning everyone and teaching everyone with all wisdom, that we may present everyone mature in Christ. For this I toil, struggling with all his energy that he powerfully works within me. For I want you to know how great a struggle I have for you and for those at Laodicea and for all who have not seen me face to face, that their hearts may be encouraged, being knit together in love, to reach all the riches of full assurance of understanding and the knowledge of God's mystery, which is Christ, in whom are hidden all the treasures of wisdom and knowledge.

COLOSSIANS 1:27–2:3

Born to Reproduce (ca. 1954)

"You can lead a soul to Christ in from 20 minutes to a couple of hours. But it takes from 20 weeks to a couple of years to get him on the road to maturity, victorious over the sins and the recurring problems that come along. He must learn how to make right decisions. He must be warned of the various 'isms' that are likely to reach out with their octopus arms and pull him in and sidetrack him. But when you get yourself a man, you have doubled your ministry—in fact, you have more than doubled your ministry. Do you know why? When you teach your man, he sees how it is done and he imitates you."

A basic technique of Bible study involves developing the skill of reading through the Bible with "lenses" on our eyes. This simple study technique involves reading prayerfully through the Bible, searching intentionally for verses and passages related to specific words, concepts, or themes. When we put on our discipleship lenses and read through the New Testament looking for passages involving teaching, learning, knowing, and understanding, it is astounding how regularly these words and themes appear in the epistles.

Words directly related to teaching, learning, and knowing appear in at least twenty-five of the ninety-five verses of the book of Colossians, and the concept of clearly understanding the things necessary for Christian maturity appears in at least twenty more verses. The whole point of this letter appears to be Paul's inspired desire to ensure that these people knew the things that he would have taught them personally if he had ministered among them.

Paul's heartfelt desire was to present *everyone*, even the saints he had never met but had only heard about, mature in Christ. Toward this end, he "toiled" and "struggled" with all of the energy and strength of Christ working within him. While Paul knew and recognized that "all the treasures of wisdom and knowledge" are *in Christ* and are available to all people who are found *in Him*, we can never personally appropriate "all the riches of full assurance of understanding" without diligent effort, careful teaching, and prayerful seeking.

Daws understood that it takes time and effort, toil and struggle, to bring baby Christians to maturity. Simply stated, making mature disciples is hard work. Children in Christ must know *that they need to be taught*, and teachers in Christ must know *what they need to teach*. Daws also saw, perhaps more clearly than anyone else of his generation, that one of the best measuring sticks of success in creating mature men and women is evidence of their ability to pour into others what had been poured into them. Paul rejoiced that he had not run in vain or labored in vain (see Philippians 2:16), because he knew that through his toil and struggle on behalf of others, the word of Christ would continue to bear fruit and grow (see Colossians 1:6) for generations to come. Daws was neither an apostle nor a prophet, but he saw clearly a basic, vital truth. Finding people and investing in them until we are able to present them fully mature in Christ is God's plan for making known the riches of the glory of the mystery of Christ.

Lord God, where are my disciples today, and what must I do to present them mature in Christ? Have I toiled and struggled with all of Your energy powerfully working within me, or have I taken a simpler, less-demanding path of allowing that to be the responsibility of someone else? Lord, all the treasures of wisdom and knowledge are found in You alone, but all these treasures must be taught and understood before they can be applied with wisdom. I pray, Lord, that You will make me a better teacher of others, so that they may be better teachers than I ever will be, so that more people may be reached with the message of Your grace than could ever be done through me alone, so that the greatness of the richness of Your glory may thereby be more clearly shown.

(KEN)

19

The Goal of Missions Is the Goal of the Great Commission

The Spirit of the Lord GOD is upon me, because the LORD has anointed me to bring good news to the poor; he has sent me to bind up the brokenhearted, to proclaim liberty to the captives, and the opening of the prison to those who are bound; to proclaim the year of the LORD's favor, and the day of vengeance of our God; to comfort all who mourn; to grant to those who mourn in Zion — to give them a beautiful headdress instead of ashes, the oil of gladness instead of mourning, the garment of praise instead of a faint spirit; that they may be called oaks of righteousness, the planting of the LORD, that he may be glorified.

ISAIAH 61:1-3

**"America," in the *King's Business*
(unknown date)**

"Our missionary work is not just getting a person to the field; that is only ten percent of the job . . ."

What was the other 90 percent of the job to which Trotman was referring? The answer is obvious by now—discipleship. Jesus said of His own ministry that His goal was to "bring good news." Trotman strove to bring the good news of Jesus Christ. He addressed the brokenhearted by introducing them to the One who gave abundant life (see John 10:10), he proclaimed "liberty" to people by reminding them of the true freedom that Christ brings (see Romans 8:2), and he comforted those who mourned by reminding them of the truth of heaven and the return of Christ.

It is true that nineteenth- and twentieth-century missions often placed more emphasis on getting to the field and less emphasis on understanding the context of the field. Some missionaries spent even less emphasis on the preparation for actual ministry in the field. It is for this reason that some contemporary conversations about missions have suggested that evangelical Christians abandon these historic models. In response to an overly cautious sense of political correctness, these conversations tend to complicate and minimize the essential missionary vision that Trotman, The Navigators, and many evangelical missionaries were trying to uphold—namely that at the heart of missions is the absolute truth of the Great Commission and the call to discipleship.

Trotman prophetically saw this tension between mission and context in the early twentieth century and wrote the *King's Business* article in response. Daws did not make a rigid distinction between "at home" church work and "over there" missionary work, choosing instead to see a continuity in ministry. In Trotman's mind, Jesus' model of ministry provided the vision for discipleship that was independent of conversations about context and culture.

Interestingly, Trotman did adjust his method in the event of contextual issues such as language barrier. For example, Navigator missionaries shared the good news in Japanese, Spanish, Hindi, and Mandarin, and eventually translated resources and books into the languages of their immediate contexts. Navigator missionaries also worked closely to understand customs and culture, oftentimes working alongside their Wycliffe Bible Translator friends. But none of the contextual requirements changed their focus on the essential message of Jesus Christ and the need for disciple-making.

Trotman's words from this article are timeless in application. Catch the vision for disciple-making. Pray for the nations. Ask the Lord to give you a context. Plant in that context. Then, bloom where you are planted. Perhaps your context is campus ministry. Go be a missionary to college students. Perhaps your context is Latin America. Go be a disciple-maker in Peru. Perhaps your context is the business world in the United States. Go make disciples in your office building.

Just remember: Ten percent of the job is locating the context. Ninety percent of the job is making disciples.

God, give us a context where we can follow Jesus in bringing good news to people. And help us to maintain Your vision for disciple-making.

(DOUG)

The Word

THE WORD

(PLACE OF)

EFFECT OBEY THEIR CAUSES BY IRRESISTABLE LAWS	WHETHER	MORAL PHYSICAL SPIRITUAL

THE WHEEL (BASIC) young fellow B.I. Prayer (
Forrey - The Word -

MUST REMEMBER

THE GOAL ⟹ A.MAN - - - - - - - -

The O.T. is the Story of what God did thru MEN -
ABRAHAM
JOSEPH
MOSES
SAMUEL - DAVID
GIDEON
DANIEL ETC.

1. A MAN AFTER OWN HEART

2. ONE TO GLORIFY.

THE LIFE
FRUIT
PRAYER
PRAISE
SUFFERING

WHAT KIND of a person -
A YIELDED LIFE

THE MEANS.

The WORD - - - - - - -

entrance

THE HAND -

		Scripture		
HEAR		Com	Com	
READ		"	"	
STUDY		"	"	
MEMORIZE		"	"	
MEDITATE		"	"	

Guidance Psa 119 105
Cleansing ⎰ John 15:5 ⎱ Psa 119:9
Conviction - HEB 4:12
Food - -
Shield - -
Sword - -

Obedience
① OBEDIENCE IN ② CONNECTION

JOHN 14:15, 21, 23
15:10, 14

172 Commandments of our Lord JESUS.

DEUT 6 -
11 -
PROV 7 -
COL 3:16

20

God Still Speaks
to His Children
Through His Word

And David became greater and greater, for the LORD, the God of hosts, was with him. And Hiram king of Tyre sent messengers to David, and cedar trees, also carpenters and masons who built David a house. And David knew that the LORD had established him king over Israel, and that he had exalted his kingdom for the sake of his people Israel.

2 SAMUEL 5:10-12

Journal Entry, March 17, 1931

"While waiting upon the Lord and reading His Word He speaks to me very definitely. I was reading II Sam the first 7 chapters. I was strangely aware that God was nigh unto me. God was, in the account in Samuel, with David for His people, Israel's, sake. II Sam. 5:10-12. David enquired many times of the Lord. I am and was then peculiarly and especially aware of mine own insufficiency and dependence upon the Lord. Chapter 7 wherein David was promised what God should verily do, burst with special significance before me. While reading the second time Heb. 6:16-18 flashed into my mind; not knowing what it was I looked up. I cannot explain how definitely the Lord spoke to me in view of the boys' [club] work in the light of America's yea the world's need. O, but that through Chap. 7, also Isa. 41:10 and Heb. 6:16-18, Rom. 4:20, 21 He did speak. I am as sure as that [William] Carey the missionary knew. I trust God, His Word, not myself nor my feelings."

This journal entry occurred during a period of great transition in Trotman's life. On the one hand, he was finishing up his last semester of education at the Bible Institute of Los Angeles, and on the other hand, like the rest of America, he was feeling the insecurity brought about by the Great Depression. Additionally, Trotman and his fiancée, Lila, were a year away from being married (1932), and Daws was taking his first steps toward organized discipleship ministry through his work with boys clubs in Lomita, a southern suburb of the emerging city of Los Angeles.

Considering that Trotman had been a Christian for only the better of five years at this point (he was converted in 1926), this journal entry is reflective of the life of a baby Christian who is still feeling his way through a formational period and who is still learning to lean on the Everlasting Arms. This was not the reflection of a mature Christian who could speak confidently and comfortably from a seasoned walk with Jesus Christ.

Notice what Trotman wrote. First, he felt "insufficient." This feeling of insecurity is quite common for new and old Christians alike. Trotman believed that one of the main tools of the Enemy (Satan) is to point out our insecurity within ourselves. Second, notice where Trotman turned—to the Bible. Daws did not turn to only one chapter or one verse but to several passages—in an effort to gain a holistic biblical perspective. He quoted from 2 Samuel and Isaiah in the Old Testament and from Romans and Hebrews in the New Testament. Third, notice the result of Trotman's turning to the Bible. He wrote that God spoke to him very definitely and was near to him. Hebrews 6:18 says that because of

God's provision, we "have strong encouragement to hold fast to the hope set before us." And Romans 4:21 says that God is "able to do what he had promised." For Trotman, these were not just promises for the New Testament church, these were promises made by God to be given to Dawson Trotman. And if Trotman were to counsel us today, he would likely remind us that God still wants to comfort us through these promises from Scripture.

God, thank You that You are bigger than our situation. Although we may find ourselves in unsettling places, Your comfort prevails because the promises of Your truth prevail. You are able to do what You have promised (Romans 4:21). And so we "have strong encouragement to hold fast to the hope set before us" (Hebrews 6:18). We thank You that You are with us, and we commit to look to Scripture as our guide in insecure and secure times alike. Amen.

(DOUG)

21

Moving from Milk
to Meat

For though by this time you ought to be teachers, you need someone to teach you again the basic principles of the oracles of God.
You need milk, not solid food, for everyone who lives on milk is unskilled in the word of righteousness; since he is a child. But solid
food is for the mature, for those who have their powers of discern-
ment trained by constant practice to distinguish good from evil.

HEBREWS 5:12-14

Journal Entry, January 6, 1937

"Ruth is getting more solid food and less milk. Just 9 months
old and we find that as she grows she must have more than just
milk. Oh if Christians would just grow with the same steadiness
that humans do. I thank God, however, for the marvelous way that
many of these Christian Service men have grown."

Many years ago, a popular TV commercial claimed that "milk does a
body good." Several passages of Scripture use the analogy of milk and
physical growth to help describe the relationship between the Word of
God and spiritual growth.

No one alive today knows for certain who wrote the epistle to the
Hebrews or to whom it was written. Apparently, it is not necessary for us

to be able to answer these questions in order to be able to understand and apply the content of the letter today. However, it is self-evident in the letter that the writer is dissatisfied with the spiritual maturity of the original recipients. It would appear that this is a fairly common problem.

This problem was also found among the people in Corinth who were "sanctified in Christ Jesus, called to be saints" (1 Corinthians 1:2), but who were not acting much like saints. According to Paul, the chief reason behind the many problems they were experiencing as a body of believers was their lack of spiritual growth and maturity as individuals. Paul had ministered among them for about eighteen months. Aquila, Priscilla, Silas, Timothy, Apollos, and Titus also ministered there. With all of those "top-notchers" in one town, Corinth should have been filled with mature believers, yet Paul repeatedly admonished them for their spiritual childishness. Apparently, the people at Corinth had become dependent upon an endless stream of gifted leaders to feed them the Word of God, and they had refused to learn how to feed themselves. The writer of Hebrews noted that the recipients of that letter were children, "unskilled in the word of righteousness." Paul offered the same complaint to the Corinthians. He wanted to address them as "spiritual people," but he could not do so.

In 1937, the work with the Navy men was still in its infancy. Daws was maturing alongside his men and his family, doing much by trial and error, but seeing fruitfulness in many places. He was learning from getting personally "down to business," from being active in his Father's business, and also from participating in the "busyness" of fatherhood. His journals recount his delight in his family and his joy in seeing his children grow. As he watched first Bruce and then Ruth move through the normal physical stages of infancy and early childhood, he learned a powerful spiritual lesson about the ministry necessity of moving people from milk to meat. Even without the help of TV commercials, he was learning that the pure spiritual milk of the Word of God was the only thing that helps a body grow in strength and maturity.

At some point, all analogies break down, and so it is here. In the physical world, people need milk in order to grow, but they soon outgrow their dependence upon it. In the spiritual world, Christians also need "milk" in order to grow, but we *never* outgrow our dependence upon it. Daws earnestly desired that the men among whom he ministered would grow with the same constancy as is evidenced in the physical realm. He understood the vital connection between milk and growth. He yearned to see the Navy men moving onward to the meatier things of God's Word. However, he also knew that a lifelong diet of the pure milk of God's Word was the key ingredient in their growth.

Lord God, we thank You and we praise You for the gift of Your Word to us. May we hunger and thirst for Your Word. May it always be better than food, better than drink, better than rest, better than anything but our relationship with You through Jesus Christ and the gift of Your Holy Spirit indwelling us. Through a steady diet of the pure milk of Your Word we grow. Without it we remain children. Give us, we pray, a passion to always be in Your Word, and spiritual wisdom and insight from Your Word, so that out of our hearts streams of the living water of Your Word may pour forth, bringing glory and honor to Your name.

(KEN)

22

The Bible and Prayer Work Together

Behold, I have refined you, but not as silver; I have tried you in the furnace of affliction. For my own sake, for my own sake, I do it, for how should my name be profaned? My glory I will not give to another.

ISAIAH 48:10-11

Journal Entry, September 16, 1939

"In the evening while on the side of the mountain, having spent a very precious and wonderful time with my Lord alone (that is, at least a couple of hours a day alone), I come to the day before our departing from this place of rest, and in no uncertain way the Lord speaks to me with reference to something that is to take place in our work. From many angles he brings scripture to my attention which makes me realize that there is a crisis ahead before long. What it is I do not know. It may be with reference to sadness as far as loved ones are concerned, or a mighty attack of Satan against the work, or something else. However, it seems the Lord is preparing me for this. After being shown several passages very clearly HE finally brings me to Isa. 48:10,11, 'Behold, I have refined thee, but not with silver; I have chosen thee in the furnace of affliction. For mine own sake ... will

99

I do it: for how should my name be polluted? and [*sic*] I will not give my glory unto another' [KJV]. This passage was most remarkable because today I had just prayed that I wanted the Lord to be glorified in whatever happened, and this passage revealed that God would be glorified in this testing. It was also given in request for a final indication from HIM that it was HIS voice speaking. The effect upon my life is not to cause me to fear in any sense of the word, but only to trust more implicitly in HIM and to lean more heavily upon HIM."

By 1939 Trotman and his Navigators were in a new period of ministry leadership. While they had not yet come into national prominence as the follow-up ministry special forces, they were nonetheless becoming well known for their incredible drive and skill in discipleship ministry. His boys and girls Scripture memory clubs were making an impact on Los Angeles area youth and his Navigators were speaking at churches, colleges, and retreats on a consistent basis. Trotman's personal speaking schedule was booked solid as Christian leaders outside of the Los Angeles area requested the discipleship guru to come challenge their organizations.

It was in thinking about these requests that Trotman wrote in September 1939. He sensed that the Lord was preparing him and his Navigators for what was to "take place in our work." He sensed that The Navigators were going to be tested and that no matter what occurred, his prayer and goal was that "God would be glorified in this testing." The result of this prayer is that Trotman learned to "lean more heavily upon Him."

Often times, Bible-centered Christians can wrongly assume that knowledge of the Bible is enough. Once we have an adequate knowledge of the Bible, we no longer *really* need to pray and seek the Lord for direction in life. Yet, Trotman's life models an important lesson for us. If anyone had reason to boast of a thorough knowledge of God's Word and the promises therein, it was Dawson Earle Trotman. One could wrongly assume that because of this knowledge, Trotman had graduated from a need to pray and seek the Lord's guidance about matters of direction and purpose. However, Trotman does not seem to suggest that the Bible was meant to replace seeking the Lord in prayer. And prayer was never meant to be a substitute for Bible study. Trotman's journal helps us to see that God uses *both* prayer and the Bible as a way to minister to us and to guide us in this life. And the result is that God is glorified more in us as we learn to trust Him.

God, thank You that You do not just give us a rule book and expect us to learn it on our own. Every step of the way You lead and guide us. In Your Word You beckon us to run with You in the race of life and to trust You each step of the way. Thank You for guiding us in Your Word and in prayer.

(DOUG)

23

The Living Water
of God's Word

Blessed is the man who walks not in the counsel of the wicked, nor stands in the way of sinners, nor sits in the seat of the scoffers; but his delight is in the law of the LORD, and on his law he meditates day and night. He is like a tree planted by steams of water that yields its fruit in its season, and its leaf does not wither. In all that he does, he prospers.

PSALM 1:1-3

S.T.S. Bible Study (ca. 1941)

"Vs. 2, Especially challenges me to meditate in the Word day and night, literally to have it on the tables of my heart that I can meditate and thus produce fruit for my GOD."

The Navigators' home base, Glen Eyrie, is located in a high desert where rainfall is unpredictable and scarce. The property sits at the confluence of two starkly different environments: a lush woodland and a dry mesa. To the west of the Glen, Camp Creek runs through Queen's Canyon and the water nourishes trees and green bamboo shoots along its banks. Just outside the eastern gates of Glen Eyrie, however, the landscape is altogether different. The arid mesa that rises up directly to the west contains no trees or bamboo shoots. Instead, the only plant life is dry grass, yucca, and prickly cacti. What accounts for the contrast? The mesa has no natural source of water.

In Psalm 1, God's Word is likened to the stream of water that nourishes the person who meditates on it daily. In our Christian life, this daily source of nourishment is vital to our flourishing. If we depart from the Word and walk in the counsel of the wicked, we will succumb to their ways and become like the desert mesa, full of prickly thorns and dead grass. If we wish to be like the green tree, however, we must have a daily intake of fresh water and light through the Scriptures.

In his AlphAmegA study on Psalm 1, Dawson Trotman challenged himself to find his delight in the law of the Lord. Trotman advocated Scripture memory as a way to produce spiritual fruit. He closed his meditation on this verse by declaring, "As a result of being obedient to God's law, to live in the Word day and night, I will be one of God's most blessed men (happy) and will always be nourished within and thus be healthy outwardly before the world."

Lord, thank You for Your nourishing Word. Please help me to delight in Your law and to meditate on it day and night. Please make me like the tree planted by the stream.

(SUSAN)

Doing the Work of God Begins with Faith in Christ

> Then they said to him, "What must we do, to be doing the works of God?" Jesus answered them, "This is the work of God, that you believe in him whom he has sent."
>
> JOHN 6:28-29

S.T.S. Bible Study (ca. late 1940/early 1941)

"It is amazing to see that God considers our real trust and faith in him the work of our lives, and yet I can see when I really believe God everything else falls into place and business is done for eternity. I must learn his Word. I must know it. I must believe it. I must let it run its full course in my life."

The Christian life is one of action verbs: witnessing, praying, preaching, and going. The one verb most important in our relationship with Christ, however, is the most powerful of all: believing. In John 6:20, Jesus reveals that, overarching all of the duties we take on, there is only one main work that Christ desires of us: to believe in Him. How radical these words must have seemed to His Jewish audience! They had spent their whole lives meticulously keeping the law of Moses and all kinds of laws their leaders had created for them over the years. It must have been quite a shock to them to hear that instead of doing all the things the law required of them, all God wanted from them was belief in the One He sent.

This comes as a shock to modern Christians too. Jesus tells His followers that the work of God is that we believe in Christ. God is the one taking on the action in this verse, not us. God will spend our entire lifetime bringing us into a deeper understanding of who He is and into a deeper faith and trust in Himself.

When we know our Creator and Sustainer and trust in His provision, everything else falls into place. We are able to obey Him because we understand that He is our Lord. We pray because we believe He is our Father who listens and cares about our needs. We witness to others because we believe that He is our Savior.

In order to know Him more deeply we must explore every avenue by which He communicates with us, especially through prayer and the Word. In his meditation on John 6, Dawson Trotman emphasized the importance of studying the Bible to gain a deeper faith and trust in God. There are four stages to Trotman's framework of studying Scripture: learning, knowing, believing, and letting the Word have influence. Learning and knowing the Word is straightforward; any eight-year-old Sunday school student can learn Bible stories and recite verses. The true Christian life starts at the believing part. We must believe that what we know of God from His Word is absolutely true, and we must let the Word sink down into our hearts and run its full course in our lives.

Jesus, I believe that You are the Christ, sent from God to redeem me. Please help me believe and know You better through Your Word.

(SUSAN)

25

Remembrance

But the Helper, the Holy Spirit, whom the Father will send in my
name, he will teach you all things and bring to your remembrance
all that I have said to you.

JOHN 14:26

S.T.S. Bible Study (ca. late 1940)

"HE shall teach you all things and bring all things to your
remembrance, whatsoever I have said unto you." So oft when I am
memorizing Scripture and writing it on the tables of my heart
and know that those passages are the Word of God, this promise
comes to my mind that HE will bring the things to my Remembrance.
The very fact of memorizing the Scripture gives HIM opportunity
to bring it back again. This HE does so often and especially in
my life or the life of another."

On January 23, 1968, North Korean soldiers boarded and captured the
U.S.S. *Pueblo* and took eighty-two crew members and officers captive.
Navy Intelligence Officer Lieutenant Stephen Harris and his fellow
sailors spent eleven months in a communist prison. For the first time in
his life, Harris found himself without access to a Bible.

In 1964, four years before the capture of the U.S.S. *Pueblo*, Harris's
chaplain introduced him to The Navigators' Topical Memory System
(TMS). Harris sent away for the TMS cards and began memorizing the

verses. He brought his Bible and verse pack with him aboard the *Pueblo* and continued studying and memorizing the Word during his surveillance assignment in the Pacific.

In early 1968 North Korea accused the *Pueblo* and her crew of spying and after a stand-off boarded the vessel in international waters. They brought the ship's six officers before a military court. Harris and the other officers received the death sentence, with the youngest officer to be shot first and the captain last. Their captors sent them to prison to await their grisly fate. During what turned out to be an eleven-month captivity marked with brutal torture and starvation, Harris and his shipmates reconstructed as much of the Bible as they could from memory. Most of the verses that Harris recalled were from the Topical Memory System. He later recalled, "Back in 1964, when I first started the memory course, I never thought I would be without access to a printed Bible!" He and his friends wrote the verses that they remembered on scraps of paper left over from the false confessions their captors forced them to write. This collection would later be called "The Pueblo Bible." The North Koreans mistook these scribbled verses for code and confiscated every sheet of paper in the cells. For the next several months the only Scripture that Harris had access to were the verses that the Lord called back to his remembrance.

After months of negotiations, the United States issued a formal statement of apology and admitted to spying activities, and the North Koreans released the prisoners. On December 23, 1968, Harris and his shipmates marched across the Bridge of No Return into South Korea. After their return home, the United States quickly rescinded its admission of spying. Harris later told his story in his book *My Anchor Holds*, in which he discussed how the Lord brought to mind the verses that he needed in the absence of the printed word.

Memorize God's Word, Christian. You will probably never languish in a communist prison cell, but there are plenty of other occasions when you will have need of a particular verse. When we have the Word written on our hearts, God will often interact with us by reminding us of qualities about Himself, and give us a warning, a word of encouragement, or a sense of direction. "He shall teach you all things, and bring all things to your remembrance" (John 14:26, KJV).

Father, please help me memorize Your Word, and write it on the tables of my heart. Please bring Your words back to my remembrance as You will and as I have need.

(SUSAN)

26

Scripture Memorization and a Transformed Life

Husbands, love your wives, as Christ loved the church and gave himself up for her, that he might sanctify her, having cleansed her by the washing of water with the word, so that he might present the church to himself in splendor, without spot or wrinkle or any such thing, that she might be holy and without blemish.

EPHESIANS 5:25-27

Journal Entry, April 13, 1945

"Norm overhears a serviceman on the train speak of the LORD. He strikes up a conversation and is finally shown a couple of letters by the fellow whose brother was found dead on the battlefields of Belgium. He was highly commended by his command-ing officer and chaplain with regards to his fine CHRISTian life. One letter spoke of finding on his body a testament and a packet of verses. They were the Topical Memory System."

While the Scripture passage above is written *to* husbands, it is *about* Christ. More specifically, these verses describe the relationship between the *will* of God in Christ in calling out a sanctified people for Himself, the *means* through which God's will is accomplished among this people, and the *result* of the application of this means to them. The key idea here is that Christ gave Himself up for His church not merely to create it but also to complete it, to bring each and every member of it to the fullness of holiness. Further, it is "the washing of water with the word" that serves as the central point of connection between God's will to sanctify His people and the eventual realization of people who actually are sanctified.

Daws clearly believed that in the process of coming to saving faith in Christ people must know they are sinners, confess their need for Christ to save them from the effects of their sins, and sincerely desire to repent of these sins. His writings demonstrate abundantly his understanding that all new followers of Christ start out this way. No one, he would argue, comes to faith in Christ *intending not to grow in holiness*. However, Daws was profoundly dissatisfied with the reality that far too many people who professed a saving relationship with Jesus Christ showed little evidence of the sanctifying work of Christ. Daws knew exactly why this was so.

Daws realized at a very early point in his ministry that while the miracle of the new birth was accomplished instantaneously at the moment of faith in, and confession of, Christ, the miracle of life trans-formation was accomplished incrementally, over time, through the care-ful and continual application of the cleansing effect of the washing of water through the Word of God. It was no accident that Navigators typi-cally demonstrated a quality of Christian life and experience that set them apart from the Christian norm. The Word of God was continually given opportunity to achieve its sanctifying effect upon them.

The journal excerpt on the previous page provides a poignant illus-tration of Ephesians 5:25-27 in action. The anonymous young soldier who died on that battlefield in Belgium was highly commended for his exemplary Christian life. Why? One clear answer is that through the ministry of The Navigators he was *in the Word of God*, possibly from the moment of his "rebirth," and definitely to the moment of his death. He died with God's Word *discovered* in his pocket. More significantly, he lived with God's Word *evident* in his life.

Lord God, Your Word itself tells us that You have given it to us so that through it we might be cleansed, transformed, washed, sanctified. Why then, Lord, do we so often neglect the very means You have provided to enable us to live as we sincerely desire to live, as children who seek to please our father? Why, Lord, do we so often fail to teach and guide other Christians with love and patience to the simple truth that their sanctification will never be found in either the wasted effort of religious legalism or in the deficient effort of passive entitlement? Thank You, Lord, for the sanctifying work of Your Word. Strengthen us, we pray, to discipline ourselves to remain under the cleansing effect of Your Word and to equip and encourage other Christians to do likewise.

(KEN)

27

Confidence in the Word of God Leads to Confidence in Evangelism

And now I commend you to God and to the word of his grace, which is able to build you up.

ACTS 20:32

"Hidden Power," in *Vision and Venture*, September 1954

"Thus the one who did not know how to witness for Christ found that the Word of God written upon his own heart was the effective instrument in reaching another life. This lad is one of thousands who have learned the value of having the living and powerful Word hidden in their hearts, that the Spirit of God may use it at a moment's notice to reach a heart for Him. [His] individual memory of Scripture had proved to be most valuable to counselor and convert alike."

Throughout all the years of his missionary journeys, Paul spent more time in Ephesus than any other place. He visited this city on two

112

separate occasions, he sent key leaders there, he raised up leaders from there, and he wrote one of the letters included in the New Testament to the believers there. During his two years in Ephesus, "all the residents of Asia heard the word of the Lord, both Jews and Greeks" (Acts 19:10). By any measure, the saints in Ephesus were blessed with an abundance of excellent equipping.

At the end of his third missionary journey, as he was heading toward Jerusalem (and eventually a Roman prison), Paul took advantage of the opportunity to have a final meeting with the elders of the Ephesian church. Among his final words to them, Paul commended them "to God and to the word of his grace, which is able to build [them] up" (Acts 20:32). Paul did not commend them into the hands of a future leader who would be able to build them up, nor did he commend them to any program, concept, or experience. He commended them to the Word of God, which was able to accomplish this task. The Word of God is living and powerful. It provides a sure and certain record of everything necessary for life and godliness. It is able to make us wise in the ways of salvation. To the extent that we "commend ourselves" to hiding God's Word in our hearts and meditating upon it, to this extent will we grow. To the limit within which we place ourselves under the discipline of the Word of God, within the constraints of this limit will we grow.

In a Bible study on John 14:26, Daws exulted in the glorious work of the Holy Spirit in using the Word of God in his life (you've already read earlier in this chapter Susan's powerful devotional on Daws' Bible study notes for this verse). As often as he saw this in his own life, however, he never ceased to be amazed at seeing the same thing happen in the lives of the men he discipled.

In this short magazine article written just two years before his death, Daws cited the example of an anonymous "lad" who was just "one of thousands" who had learned that memorizing Scripture was the best way to be prepared at all times to make a defense to anyone who asked the reason for the hope that was in him. It was the best way in 1954, and it remains the best way still today. Let us commend one another to the Word of God, which is able to build us up in Christ's grace.

Lord God, nearly two thousand years ago Your servant Paul commended a group of dedicated, discipled saints to You and to the word of Your grace. These men, who were already mightily built up by Your Spirit and by other believers, were instructed to continue to be built up through Your Word. We thank You for their example, and we thank You for the lesson from the life of this anonymous "lad" who was enabled to reach another life with the message of Your grace. Though he "did not know how to witness for Christ," he was taught how to memorize Scripture. May we continue to hide Your Word in our hearts, and may You use our diligence to Your glory.

(KEN)

July 29 1947

PACE SETTING

HEB 11

The Living Embodiment
of your message

Moss. 40 years
David —

PREACH BY LIFE
II COR. 2nd
3rd
4th
5th
6th
7th Titus.
8th — MACEDONION.

II Cor 8:11

A Nav. Principle
ITS IN THE
WORD

DEFINE
WHEEL —
HAND
~~WHEEL~~
FOLLOW UP.
BALANCE
PACE SETTING

WHY DO
WE CALL
NAV Pric

Command Teach!   I Tim 4:11,12
but ---

GREATEST HUMAN ---   I Tim 1:16
Phil 1:—
II COR 11—

Watch him in Action   I Thes—
II Tim 4:7,8. Fight.

So he could Challenge   Phil 4:9.
I Cor 11:1

The GREAT PACE SETTER.   Heb 12:3.

Call   LUKE 4:23 because Heb 5:8

I Pet 2:21

IN PRAYER
Watch Him. in
Glorify

OTHERS --- Phil 2:3,4,5
Rom 15:3

Comforting - Night before +
John 14:1

THE Lost. { Mat 9:36-38

Life before men   Luke 2:52
Temptation -- Heb 2:18 4,15 Mat 4.
TRIAL — accused— { (Rua) not again
{ Isa
ON the Cross — mother- father forgiv.
The Servant — .. John 13
Humility — An Ass —
Sorrow ... John 14 —
Suffering Heb 5:9,10
the Sheep   99 - 1

28

Mature Christians Should Be "Pacesetters" in Scripture Intake

Brothers, join in imitating me, and keep your eyes on those who walk according to the example you have in us.

PHILIPPIANS 3:17

Power to Re-Create (ca. 1953)

"Many Christians who love God and seek to serve Him are yet content to live on the ten to twenty verses of Scripture that they have known for that many years. Is the new Christian who enters your church and the family of God to have such an example set before him? Or is he to find Christians who are regularly reading and studying the Word of God and writing it on their hearts?"

Almost every parent notices at some point that his children watch him closely and that they often very intentionally mimic what their parent does. Most parents can likely remember a time when they caught their children awkwardly attempting to use words or phrases they commonly use, retelling their old, tired jokes, learning to eat (and pretending to enjoy) food that they eat, voicing opinions on matters they could not possibly understand, and even developing many of their parents' physical habits and mannerisms.

Anyone who leads in ministry has likewise probably observed that the people he serves watch him closely and often mimic what he does. Leaders should be gratified when people copy their good behaviors (and grieved when they copy their bad ones). If leaders make a habit of reading through the Bible every year, over time more and more people begin to do likewise. If leaders are diligent in the discipline of Scripture memorization, other people will copy this practice. If leaders always try to answer questions from Scripture rather than from simple experience or emotion, other people will begin to learn to do the same thing.

In Philippians 3:17, Paul exhorted the church at Philippi with two commands: to be intentional in choosing to join others in imitating him (Greek, Συμμιμηται, which literally means "to become fellow-imitators"), and to take special notice of those people who were already imitating his example. While this passage relates in a broad, general way to the conduct of life issues, the two commands in this verse can and must apply with equal validity to the specific individual practices of Scripture intake and memorization, as it is only by placing ourselves under the authority of the Word of God that we can begin to understand what it means to be transformed into the image of the Son of God.

In typical Daws fashion, the excerpt cited from his message *Power to Re-Create* contains strong words of warning, conviction, and challenge. First, he noted that many Christians are not "setting the pace" in ongoing growth in their knowledge of the Word of God. He observed that many people start well in memorizing and actually learning to rightly handle ten or twenty (or some other arbitrary number) of Bible verses, but that this practice tends to slow quickly and then cease entirely in the lives of many Christians. This, by itself, is a troubling truth. Second, however, he noted that our "church children" are carefully observing us and that many of them are intentionally copying the pattern they are seeing in us. The questions Daws asked some seventy years ago deserve to be asked again, and indeed they *demand* being asked again, to the churches of today. What example are the new Christians who enter our church to find set before them? Are they to find coasting Christians who are content to live for decades on the handful of Bible verses and concepts they encountered in some bygone time? Or, are they to find Christians who regularly and systematically read and study God's Word? What legacy of behavior will our own actions create in and for the next generation of Christians?

Lord, help us, we pray, in three things. First, Lord, give us conviction of spirit regarding our need to be faithful and diligent in reading, studying, memorizing, and learning Your Word so that it may be written on our hearts with ever-increasing clarity and force. Second, Lord, give us strength to be diligent in persevering in the practice of being daily in Your Word. Third, Lord, give us spiritual eyes to see that younger Christians are observing, and often copying, the example that we are setting. May we be able, with personal confidence, to say to saints who surround us what Paul said to the saints who were at Philippi: "Join others in imitating me and keep Your eyes on those people who copy the example that I am setting."

(KEN)

Prayer

29

Prayer Leads
to Purpose

As soon as I heard these words I sat down and wept and mourned for days, and I continued fasting and praying before the God of heaven.

NEHEMIAH 1:4

Journal Entry, August 21, 1929

"Beginning of Journal of Dawson E. Trotman: Time spent alone in hills in confession of sin and spiritual renewal."

At the time of the events related in the first verses of the book of Nehemiah, some of the people of Israel were living in exile in Babylon and some were living in their homeland. Nehemiah was among the exiles in Babylon, serving the king in the city of Susa. Word came to him there of the wretched condition of the remnant of Israel living in Jerusalem. In response, Nehemiah spent days weeping and mourning, fasting and praying. Out of this season of prayer, God revealed Himself to Nehemiah and shaped him as a leader able to help restore fallen Israel.

There are three potential orderings of the relationship between going to God in prayer and hearing a clear word from God. First, God can reveal His will for us entirely on His own initiative. God revealed His will to Abram in Ur (Genesis 12), He revealed His will to Moses in the desert (Exodus 3), and He revealed His will to Paul on the road to Damascus (Acts 9). In each of these instances, there is nothing in the text to indicate that these people were seeking God's will or direction.

Second, God could reveal His will for us in a way that adds confirmation for, or detail about, a decision or plan we have already made. There are few biblical examples of God's revealing Himself and His will in this manner, but this method seems to be the one most commonly followed by Christians today in seeking to determine God's will. Perhaps one might say that bringing our supplications and requests to God in prayer falls under this practice, but our widespread habit of "putting out a fleece" would benefit by a closer examination of Judges 6:36.

Third, God can reveal His will for us during or after times of prayer, when our hearts are open to whatever He might choose to put in them. The angel Gabriel appeared and revealed God's will while Daniel was in prayer (Daniel 9:20-21). Cornelius received a word from God while in prayer (Acts 10:30). During a season of fasting and worship, God revealed His will regarding Barnabas and Saul (Acts 13:2). This ordering, with *prayer leading to purpose*, seems to be the one most commonly found throughout the Bible.

The very first entry Daws made in his journal states simply, "Time spent alone in hills in confession of sin and spiritual renewal." Over the course of the next twenty-seven years, across more than 1,300 individual journal entries, the most common topic Daws mentions is prayer. He recorded times spent in prayer, he agonized over specific items of prayer, and he rejoiced in answers to prayers. It was through long seasons of prayer that God's purpose for Daws and for the work he was eventually to do through The Navigators became clear.

Many people claim to have discovered the so-called secret of prayer, but the secret can be simplified to the one word, *pray*. Anyone can possess much Bible knowledge, but it is impossible to be mighty in the Word of God without being mighty in prayer as well. It is no coincidence that Daws' journal begins with and is saturated with prayer, and that The Navigators accomplished so much that was mighty in God's sight. Even before there was the Wheel, one of "the three legs of the stool" (Daws' first illustration of the Christian life) was prayer. In our zeal to be people of the Word, let us never forget that we must also be people of prayer.

Lord God, keep us ever mindful that we will never do anything of eternal significance without fervent, abundant prayer. In the "journal of our lives," may the most noticeable aspect be its saturation with themes of prayer. In the legacy we leave behind, may it be known that we were people of much prayer. As we seek Your face in prayer, we trust in You to guide us according to Your will, that we might see and fulfill Your every purpose.

(KEN)

30

The Discipline of Prayer Empowers Ministry

Continue steadfastly in prayer, being watchful in it with thanksgiving. At the same time, pray also for us, that God may open to us a door for the word, to declare the mystery of Christ, on account of which I am in prison — that I may make it clear, which is how I ought to speak.

COLOSSIANS 4:2-4

Journal Entry, August 30, 1929

"I went to the old church about 9:00 p.m. and prayed until I could stay awake no longer and laid down on the floor and slept until daybreak at what time I again poured out my heart before the Lord."

Journal Entry, April 7, 1931

"Oh the conflicts of my soul as I try to pray! Shall I let God use me. I must learn to pray, to wrestle by the hour for souls.

Oh Jehovah—catch me, hold me, strengthen me. I need Thee every moment."

How often and for how long should a Christian pray? For the majority of Christians, the answer is probably, "More frequently and for longer periods of time than I do at present." It certainly is convicting to compare the biblical instructions and examples regarding God's will for our frequency in, and duration of, personal prayer with our actual experiences in the ongoing practice of prayer.

In Colossians 4:2, the word translated in the English Standard Version as "continue steadfastly in" is a word of command, not of suggestion (Greek, προσκαρτερεῖτε). As it is used in this particular phrase, it carries the idea of adhering to or being constant toward something—in this case, prayer. If this were the only place where Scripture commands obedience to the ongoing practice of prayer, we might well miss the significance of it, but such is not the case.

On the contrary, Scripture *abounds* with commands to continue steadfastly in prayer. We are commanded to "pray without ceasing" (1 Thessalonians 5:17) and to pray "at all times . . . with all prayer and supplication" (Ephesians 6:18). Scripture also abounds with examples of people who prayed "continuously." In the Old Testament, Nehemiah affirmed that he prayed "day and night" for Israel (Nehemiah 1:6), and Daniel had a habit of praying three times each day (see Daniel 6:10). In the New Testament, Paul cited his own example of having "not ceased" in his habits of praying for people (see Ephesians 1:16; Colossians 1:9), and one test of spiritual fitness is that a person be known as someone who "continues in supplications and prayers night and day" (1 Timothy 5:5). In addition, Jesus spent time regularly in prayer (see Luke 5:16), and He also observed extended periods of prayer (see Luke 6:12).

The latest reliable surveys indicate that the average Christian in America spends about *five minutes* each day in prayer. Pastors, it appears, are far more average than we might wish, claiming to spend about seven minutes each day in prayer. Need we look further in seeking an answer for why our churches seem to lack power, and why Christians so often struggle to overcome sin in their lives?

In the earliest years of his Christian life, when he first felt himself drawn to service for Christ, Daws struggled mightily to develop habits of regular *and* extended prayer. The excerpt from his journal in 1929 is one of many such entries in which he recorded the experience of his efforts to spend whole "days and nights" (and sometimes weeks and months) in prayer. The important point to observe is not whether Daws succeeded or failed in completing a planned prayer vigil, and not whether he received the "word from God" he was looking for as he prayed. Rather, the most important point in these many journal entries is that from an early stage of his Christian experience Daws disciplined himself to the habitual practice of regular and extended prayer. Nearly two years later, in the 1931 entry, we see that Daws still felt the need to "learn to pray," but at least he was still working at it diligently.

Lord, not one of us is able to pray as we should, and so we thank You for the gift of Your Holy Spirit, who searches our hearts and prays perfectly for us every prayer that should be prayed and every prayer that is prayed. May our recognition of this work of Your Holy Spirit never allow us to become lazy or neglectful in our habits of prayer. Help us, Lord, to pray with more frequency, with more urgency, and with more attention to the needs of the world in which we live. Help us to discipline ourselves to spend more time in prayer, not just because You command us to do so, and not just because You have given us good examples to follow, but because our hearts truly yearn to be in closer communion with You, and ever more so, and ever more so, and ever more so!

(KEN)

31

The Habit of Prayer Requires Discipline

Now Jesus was praying in a certain place, and when he finished, one of his disciples said to him, "Lord, teach us to pray, as John taught his disciples."

LUKE 11:1

Journal Entry, July 14, 1931

"I find the hardest thing for me to do is to get to prayer. God is able to make me a man of prayer if it pleases Him."

Men of prayer do not appear to be born that way. In the case of Jesus' disciples, this certainly seems to be true. These men had grown up in the synagogue, had participated in the ritual festivals at Jerusalem, had journeyed far from home to personally witness the ministry of John the Baptist, and finally, they had committed themselves to the demands of becoming disciples of Jesus. They were not strangers to the world of prayer. They had been exposed to prayer throughout the entirety of their lives, but exposure to prayer had not made them men of prayer.

Most New Testament scholars agree that Luke's gospel is constructed thematically rather than chronologically, making it difficult to date with certainty many events in relation to the years of the public ministry of Jesus. However, regardless of whether the disciples had been with Jesus for three months or for three years when they asked His advice on prayer, three things are clear from this one verse of Scripture. First, the disciples had been with Jesus long enough for them to have observed His habits of prayer and to have built up confidence in His standing as a teacher and leader. Second, even though all the young men of Israel grew up within a culture filled with ritual prayer in home and synagogue and temple, both the disciples of John and the disciples of Jesus needed specific teaching and training in prayer as part of the "discipling" process. Third, the disciples of Jesus were aware enough that their prayer lives needed this help to ask for it.

In the middle of 1931, Daws was still a young Christian in many respects, but he was maturing quickly. He was already "down to business" in regular memorization of Scripture, he was active in the "personal work" of evangelism, and he was busy organizing Fisherman's Clubs in and around Lomita. He had also begun to establish the habit of spending extended times in prayer, both alone and with other men.

This journal entry appears directly below one of the earliest ink drawings of the Wheel. Of the four spokes of the Wheel (prayer, witnessing, word, and fellowship), Daws observed in himself that "the hardest thing for me to get to is prayer." In a journal entry for April 1 of that year he had written simply, "Prayerless—I struggle." Less than a week later, on April 6, he noted that he spent the entire day in prayer. The very next day he lamented, "I must learn to pray." Over the next several months, Daws learned to discipline himself to prayer through hours and hours out on "the hill," alone with God or in the fellowship of like-minded men of God. His journals show that he continued to feel that prayer was the "hardest thing . . . to get to," but he persevered in practicing the discipline of regular prayer, and over time, he became a man of prayer.

All true disciples of Jesus, it appears, eventually come to the point of crying out, "Lord, teach me to pray! I, too, need help!" One of the ways we come to this realization is by observing the prayers and the prayer habits of Jesus. Another way is by observing mature Christians who consistently model a life of richness and depth in prayer. Instruction and accountability in prayer serve as one of the spokes of the Navigator Wheel, and deservedly so. Prayer is one of the four vital points of connection and support between "Christ the Center" and "The Obedient Christian in Action." Daws learned this lesson early, and it became a staple of the Navigator disciple-making method.

Lord God, teach us to pray! You are able to make us men and women of prayer, for this does please You. May You convict our hearts regarding our habits of "prayerlessness," for when prayer is absent we struggle. May You reveal to our hearts our rituals of powerless and ineffectual prayer. We long for and need Your help in teaching us to pray with passion, with boldness, with strength, and with confidence.

(KEN)

32

We Go Forward in God's Word as We Go Forward in Prayer

His master said to him, "Well done, good and faithful servant. You have been faithful over a little; I will set you over much. Enter into the joy of your master."

MATTHEW 25:21

Journal Entry, April 22, 1932

"We were led to take this time for prayer, meeting at 11 o'clock in the Lomita church. Before we could ask GOD's blessing for his work we felt that we needed to be in the place of blessing ourselves and so we spent the first few minutes in searching our hearts and in confessing our sins and shortcomings. We do thank GOD that forgiveness and deliverance from sin does not depend on long repetitive prayers, but on simple faith in GOD's cleansing grace, as sins are confessed and the heart longs and expects deliverance. We also thank Him that we reviewed again another secret of victory seen in yielding our members as instruments of righteousness to the Holy Spirit. We asked for victory over the failure to do those things that we knew we should do in our own

lives. And having asked in faith we expect to see it. . . .
Following this we consider the future work of the Fisherman's
Club and realizing the great need of a great work done for GOD,
in His power, and for His glory, we asked Him to touch 2 million
young people through us. In considering the boys' work we saw
that counting all Prospectors and Junior Fisherman possible we
could account for only 200 in clubs. This led us to ask for
1000. . . . We thank GOD for teaching us that we can only go
forward in the work as we go forward in prayer and we long for
more of such prayer meetings as this one."

In 1932 Dawson Trotman was a six-year-old Christian, a newly married
man, a recent college grad, and an attendant at a gas station during the
Great Depression. If asked, Trotman would have gushed about his situation in life. He was content. One of the main reasons for his godly
contentment was the over-availability for discipleship ministry within
his local context. Trotman was meeting with at least three sailors for
Bible study and evangelism training. He was also leading at least two
children's and youth Bible study and Scripture memory clubs in the
Lomita area. Interestingly, Trotman viewed these ministry opportunities
as personal disciplines within his lay-ministry identity. In addition to
each of these lay ministries, Trotman was also a part-time pastor for a
local Bible church in Southern California.

In all of this, Trotman was content. Although living in an abandoned garage behind the gas station where he worked, Trotman and Lila
were content in their dwelling space. Although he had to meet with the
sailors for Bible study in a gasoline shed, Trotman and his sailors were
content. And although his church plant was still reeling from the funda-
mentalist/modernist split in 1931, they were content. The question
arises as to how Trotman and his people were so content during this
tumultuous time period. And the answer is located in his journals.

God taught him that Christians "can only go forward in the work as
we go forward in prayer."

Because Trotman disciplined himself to spend time daily in prayer, he had an overflowing and satisfying prayer life. And because he had a satisfying prayer life, Trotman experienced a satisfying ministry life. Jesus told a parable in Matthew 25 that illuminates Trotman's journal entry. A master gave talents (a monetary unit that was equal to about twenty years' wages) to several laborers, and the faithful laborers put them to use. The result? Not only were the laborers able to increase their talents, but they also were granted additional responsibilities and entered into the joy of the master.

Again, how were Trotman and his people so content during this tumultuous time period? They were faithful to pray and put the Bible into practice. The Lord produced spiritual dividends and brought them satisfying joy and contentment. And in addition, the ministry opportunities grew. The rest of the story between 1932 and 1956 is that the three sailors and youth Bible clubs transformed into The Navigators organization and Trotman became the catalyst for the American discipleship movement. Yet, journal entries confirm that no matter how successful Trotman became, his joy remained solely fixed on God in prayer. Prayer was the source and expression of his contentment.

God, I long to be a faithful servant with the talents that You graciously give to me. I long only to put them into practice and receive the joy of the Master. You do what You want with the talents. I will follow You and find my contentment in You.

(DOUG)

33

Morning Prayer

Satisfy us in the morning with your steadfast love, that we may
rejoice and be glad all our days.

PSALM 90:14

Journal Entry, January 9, 1939

"Up Early and have Devotions with Lila. We are fighting through
to have this time with the Lord each morning. Strange how easily
Christians are sidetracked from the things that are known to be
essential. We have both felt it very much in our two lives that
is the lack of this time together."

By 1939, Dawson and Lila had plenty of things to sidetrack them from
their morning devotions. Young Bruce and Ruthie competed for their
parents' attention. Their three-bedroom home at 4845 bustled with
activity every hour of the day. At least three evenings a week sailors from
the local Navy base came over for dinner and Bible study. On Saturday
the visitors would play volleyball, football, and ping-pong. The sailors
with liberty for the weekend often stayed the night, sleeping on sofas in
the living room, cots in the garage, and up in the loft. On such nights,
the four Trotmans slept on mattresses in one room.

With so much activity in the house, Daws and Lila struggled to find
time as a couple to meet with the Lord together. Dawson recognized the
importance of the morning family devotions that Dietrich Bonhoeffer

advocated. Despite the busyness of their lives, Dawson and Lila made a point to continue meeting with the Lord early in the day. Morning prayer set the tone of their entire day and feasting on the Word in the early light stayed their minds on Christ.

Christian, do you struggle with finding time to meet with God in the morning? Fight through to have this time. Regardless of how many lives you must save in the operating room, how many students await you in the classroom, or how many small mouths you must feed today, spending time with your heavenly Father is the most important work you can do. In Luke 10:38-42, Martha is busy serving Christ and their guests. When she sees her sister Mary sitting down and listening, rather than working, she becomes annoyed and complains to Jesus. He responds, "Martha, Martha, you are anxious and troubled about many things, but one thing is necessary. Mary has chosen the good portion, which will not be taken away from her" (verses 41-42).

Before you begin serving the people in your charge, whether spouse and children, or employer, sit at the feet of Christ for a while. Even if this quiet time is in your room before you rise, meet with the Lord. It's okay if the bulk of your study in the Word occurs later in the day. Just greet Christ in the morning and attune your heart to hear from Him all day.

Lord, please have the first word with me in the morning. Please help me greet You with joy each day and to spend time with You before doing anything else.

(SUSAN)

34

Daws Dared to Pray Large Prayers

You do not have, because you do not ask.

AlphAmegA Bible Study, Psalm 2 (ca. 1942)

"Here [in verse 8] GOD says, 'Ask of me and I shall give thee the heathen for thine inheritance' [KJV]. GOD gives much without our asking, for HE knows our needs. But here HE challenges me to ask for one of the greatest things in all the world, the souls of heathen people."

How "large" should Christians dare to pray? According to the witness of the Gospels, as large as our minds can conceive, so long as we are in Christ and praying according to His will.

Jesus regularly admonished His disciples to pray for *anything* in His name. In the Sermon on the Mount, Jesus said, "Ask, and it will be given" (Matthew 7:7). The same words appear a second time, in a different setting, in Luke's gospel (Luke 11:9). Both Matthew and Mark give us the message of Jesus' saying, "Whatever you ask in prayer, you will receive, if you have faith" (Matthew 21:22; see also Mark 11:24). John's gospel records several instances of Jesus' having spoken these and similar words, including the statement, "If you abide in me, and my words abide in you, ask whatever you wish, and it will be done for you" (John 15:7).

James tells us bluntly that there are two reasons we do not have what we ask for in prayer. One reason is that we ask wrongly, from selfish motives, according to our own will and not according to the will of God (see James 4:3). The other reason we do not have is quite simply because we do not ask (see James 4:2). What makes us so timid in our asking?

Daws regularly exhorted Navigators to pray God-sized prayers. In several of his messages he challenged his listeners to pray for entire continents instead of just neighborhoods, and to take God at His word, trusting in His promises to give us whatever we ask in His name. He mentioned these themes directly in *Call unto Me*, *The Need of the Hour*, and *The Big Dipper*.

In this early AlphAmegA Bible study (perhaps 1940 or 1941), Daws was on what was, for him, familiar ground, reading Old Testament promises as if God were speaking the words directly to and for him personally. The psalmist wrote, "I will tell of the decree: The LORD said to me, 'You are my Son; today I have begotten you. Ask of me, and I will make the nations your heritage, and the ends of the earth your possession'" (Psalm 2:7-8).

Daws took God at His word here, as elsewhere. Because he considered himself a child begotten of God, he saw no reason to lack faith that this promise from God was meant for him. He sincerely believed that praying for the souls of men was in the will of God, and he therefore believed just as ardently that it was impossible for him to out-ask God's ability to answer prayer in this regard.

Lord God, You are infinitely great beyond every limit of our comprehension, Your Word is gloriously magnificent in its unbounded promises to us, and Your power is eternally able to fulfill every promise of Yours to the uttermost extent, and yet our prayers are so shallow and so small! We confess, Lord, that we too often fail to receive because we fail to ask, and that we too often fail to ask because we fail to believe that You will answer out of the abundance of Your love and in the fullness of Your might. Help us, Lord, to pray for continents instead of just cul-de-sacs, for entire peoples instead of just people, for the furthest limits of the world instead of just our friends next door. While we recognize that every soul is precious, and that even "small prayers" are large in Your love, encourage us, Lord, to "pray large" more often, and to trust You with full confidence that You will gladly give us whatever we ask in Your name.

(KEN)

35

Workers in
the Harvest

Then he said to his disciples, "The harvest is plentiful, but the laborers are few; therefore pray earnestly to the Lord of the harvest to
send out laborers into his harvest."

MATTHEW 9:37-38

Journal Entry, December 7, 1944

"Wonderful time on the hill last night. Asked the Lord that he
might work in the hearts of high school, college kids, or business people to the end that in years to come HE would give us
out of the whole US top-notchers for the work He is going to do
through The Navigators. Might just as well put it down in my book
now that it is a settled matter, the Lord accepted my request.
It is on His books and on the way."

On December 6, 1944, Dawson Trotman left his home after dinner to
climb the bluffs behind his home at 509 Monterey Road. He took his
jacket, Bible, and a Navy blanket and climbed the hill to a favorite spot
where he could see the city lights.

After reflecting on the new staff members that the Lord had brought
The Navigators, he began to pray for future generations of laborers.
Dawson's work in boys and girls Bible clubs and at BIOLA had taught

him the importance of training youth, and he was beginning to see the fruits of his ministry. That December night he prayed that the Lord would raise up young laborers for the field, and he was confident that the Lord would do it.

More than sixty-five years later, it is easy to see how faithfully and abundantly God answered Trotman's prayer on the hill behind his house. The staff of The Navigators has grown from 4 in 1944 to over 4,800 in 2011. The Navigators has laborers all over the globe, in 108 countries.

"Top-notchers" in their respective fields have left their previous jobs and schooling to use their talents in the ministry. For example, after coming to Christ, expert businessman Donald McGilchrist left his coveted position with British Rail in the United Kingdom to join The Navigators. He has been with the organization for forty years as of April 2011 and is using his business and theological acumen to reach people around the world for Christ. If you are reading this passage and you are a member of The Navigators, you are part of God's answer to Trotman's prayer. God has worked in your heart and has brought you to The Navigators to reach people for Himself.

In 2011 The Navigators' collegiate work ministers to students at campuses across the country. The students who graduate from universities with Navigator ministries are invited to join Edge Corps, an opportunity for young graduates to come on staff and labor alongside the larger organization. The Lord is at work in the hearts of future generations who will continue to serve Him in the context of the Navigator work.

In Matthew 9:37-38, Christ asked us to pray for laborers for the harvest. We have seen Him bless The Navigators with faithful laborers for the kingdom. Will you join us in praying that He continues to raise up future generations who will go into the fields of harvest?

Lord, please work in the hearts of high school students, university undergrads and graduate students, and your businesspeople to raise up top-notch laborers for Your kingdom.

(SUSAN)

36

Through Prayer God Prepares Us for Discipleship

Pray without ceasing.

1 THESSALONIANS 5:17

Westmont College Seminar, July 20, 1951

"In brief you know that in a 40 day period in which I met the Lord for two hours each morning with another fella and three [hours] on Sunday, [from] four o'clock in the morning till seven [o'clock]. I was sleepy, [for] sure. I had to battle [sleepiness] every morning to get up there and we met the Lord on the dot at five [o'clock].

"We spread our little list of names of the couple of hundred boys that had accepted Christ in our community, prayed for them one by one, prayed for the little towns around us. . . . And as we prayed morning after morning and began to reach out in the United States . . . really we thought we were prayin big. . . . And honest gang, as I remember it we really were breathing hard when we started to pray that God would give us the privilege of leading young men to Christ from every state in the union. . . .

That last week we decided to pray that God would give us men in the whole world; and we took a map of the world and put our fingers on Australia and Europe and Asia and Africa. . . . It hadn't come to (sic) clearly to mind what we wanted, but we were praying definitely one thing.

"And you know, I'm surely glad the Lord led us to pray that. [Because] God gave us men.

"I didn't realize that prayer is the heart of this whole thing."

In his 1951 Navigator Conference speech, Trotman was making reference to his 1931 prayer experiment. Trotman dedicated forty days in March and April 1931 to the task of praying for the nations toward the spiritual goal of global evangelism and salvation. Because Trotman was about the task of mentoring at this point, he regularly invited friends and his "Timothys" to join him in prayer for the nations. Many Trotman biographers consider this forty-day prayer experiment the genesis for the modern Navigator and discipleship movements.

Trotman's own personal practice of spiritual disciplines consisted of early morning prayer—a discipline that he maintained throughout his life. Trotman was also somewhat of an outdoorsman and enjoyed listening to God while in nature. His routine in the early 1930s was to drive to the hills above Redondo Beach and pray while looking over Southern California. This was the spot where Trotman heard clearly from the Lord.

By 1951, The Navigators was an established and well-oiled machine of a ministry and the annual conference served as a yearly huddle where Trotman could rally the troops and remind them of the task at hand. It is significant to reflect on the content of this particular sermon.

Trotman's call to prayer was not a novel teaching—The Navigators knew that prayer was one of the six components of the Wheel illustration. Trotman's speech was a reminder that prayer was not only the origin of God's work in The Navigators, but also the sustaining force and the future of The Navigators.

Trotman firmly believed that the idea for discipleship and The Navigators originated in the heart of God, and thus Trotman's singular goal in leadership was to find out God's plan of action and then to obey His orders. If there is anything that Christians can take away from the 1951 speech, it is that nothing has changed in God's game plan. He still wants us to get our marching orders from Him through a quality time of prayer and then to act accordingly in obedience.

God, we are listening. Speak to us and tell us what You want us to do. And thank You for Your Bible, which helps us to hear You better.

(DOUG)

Fellowship

37.

Human Heart Struggles and a Holy God

For we know that the law is spiritual, but I am of the flesh, sold under sin. For I do not understand my own actions. For I do not do what I want, but I do the very thing I hate. Now if I do what I do not want, I agree with the law, that it is good. So now it is no longer I who do it, but sin that dwells within me. For I know that nothing good dwells in me, that is, in my flesh. For I have the desire to do what is right, but not the ability to carry it out. For I do not do the good I want, but the evil I do not want is what I keep on doing. Now if I do what I do not want, it is no longer I who do it, but sin that dwells within me.

ROMANS 7:14-20

Journal Entry, January 12, 1937

"Today, while reading 'Bush Aglow' my heart is tremendously stirred. I see so many things happening in this man's life that are like events of my own that I am strengthened as I realized that others whom God has used have had the same heart struggles that I have. Paul in Rom 7 speaks of this but it seems to bring it so near to me to read concerning the life of one of His servants who lived such a short time ago. It has been so long since my heart condition has moved me to tears, but these came as I saw the sinfulness of my life in view of the Holyness [*sic*] of God and the preciousness of souls."

Sin is not a popular topic in Christian conversations, sermons, speeches, and literature in the twenty-first century. Some pastors have suggested that postmodern audiences do not respond to or even understand the concept of sin and sinfulness. Other authors have suggested a moratorium on conversations about sin and sinfulness. Sin is not a comfortable topic—a notion that guides much of what is talked about in popular radio and print conversations about Christianity and the Christian life in general. If one were to create a poll on the topic, it is likely that the larger American population would find sin to be fading from a top-ten list of important Christian issues, being edged out by items such as poverty, worship music, social justice, needs in Africa, and matters of biblical interpretation.

In many ways, the twenty-first century is not too different from the early twentieth century when Trotman was alive and writing. This journal entry from 1937 comes during the Sophistication Period of Trotman's life. His Navigators were an established and growing ministry with a particular ministry mission and focus. His family was growing with the addition of children and subsequent moves to bigger homes. And, his personal spiritual life was at a thriving point with 1937 and 1938 producing the highest number of journal entries in Trotman's journal collection.

However, Trotman was keenly aware that his ministry and life success did not change a fundamental and paradoxical fact—God is holy and Trotman is still human and sinful. While reading the devotional biography of Dwight L. Moody titled *Bush Aglow*, written by Richard Day, Trotman was reminded of something that was consistent in the nineteenth century in Moody's time—God is holy and man is human and sinful. This reminder of the paradoxical nature of our existence drove Trotman to remember what was true in the apostle Paul's day—God is holy and man is human and sinful.

One can observe a not-so-coincidental trend in postmodern American society. Christians who desire to lessen an emphasis on the doctrine of sin and humanity also tend to be the same Christians who refrain from teaching on the fundamental attributes of God, especially His holiness. When one is kept from being reminded about God's holiness, one fails to see oneself in comparison with a holy God and by contrast, one's own imperfection and sinfulness. The result of this program of teaching (or nonteaching) is that one is allowed to falsely presume a reality void of truth.

Dawson Trotman reminded us that what was true for the apostle Paul in the first century was true for Moody and for Trotman and for us today. Man is sinful. God is holy. The tension is and should be there. It is the tension that affords an opportunity for sharing the good news that Jesus Christ died to resolve that tension and to bring man into a saving relationship with God. This is the foundation for discipleship because God graciously continues to desire a relationship with a sinful, yet progressively sanctified humanity.

God, thank You for loving a sinful people and graciously giving us Your gift in Jesus Christ. Help us to be people who stay gospel-centered in all that we say, think, and do.

(DOUG)

38

The Lord Is the Source of Fellowship

Behold, I am doing a new thing; now it springs forth, do you not perceive it? I will make a way in the wilderness and rivers in the desert.

ISAIAH 43:19

So they shall fear the name of the LORD from the west, and his glory from the rising of the sun; for he will come like a rushing stream, which the wind of the LORD drives.

ISAIAH 59:19

Whatever you do, work heartily, as for the Lord.

COLOSSIANS 3:23

Journal Entry, April 10, 1937

"This is to be our last Saturday night in 1114 Pacific. Announcement is made of our future course in how the Lord has indicated for us to move. I have not time here to tell how wonderfully the Lord led in the matter but only to say that though we are going out where we know not yet He is very definitely leading and time will show what great things the Lord will do for us. Isaiah 43:19

"We have a goodly meeting. Quartet is down, also Bob Rogers the man that Gurney [Harris] led to the Lord up in the slums of the LA.

"Several stay over so that they might help in the meeting at DeGroff's tomorrow. Mainly Norton, Jowers, Bell, Johansson.

"Norton is now leading the song services and growing.

"Oh how wonderful for brethren dwell together in Unity and the Lord has given us such a bond of Love and fellowship together these days. We can see how the enemy has endeavored to wreck/but God. Isaiah 59:19"

A key trait of younger evangelical Christians is a high relational skill set. In other words, younger evangelicals are exceptionally social animals. This is one reason, social commentators suggest, for the expansion and mass growth of social networking, blogs, and electronic communications. Text messages, Facebook, Twitter, e-mail, chat rooms, and comment features share one key characteristic—they are all driven by a social appetite and relational need.

An influential pastor recently remarked that many of the advantages of modern and postmodern American society that were initially projected to advance the gospel have in effect hindered the gospel in this generation. This generation of Christians is wealthier per capita than any previous American generation and yet spends less per capita on foreign and domestic mission projects. This generation is more educated and yet the baby boomer pastors are beginning to retire with a general panic as to replacement pastors. This generation is technologically superior and yet has not used that technology to preach the gospel to remote parts of the globe. Likewise, this generation is ridiculously gifted in relationship building and yet fails time and again to leverage the gospel into relationships.

This journal entry from April 1937 illustrates two paradigmatic features of Trotman's thinking. First, he heavily quoted from Isaiah and claimed these texts as promises from God to The Navigators. Trotman loved quoting and pulling promises from Isaiah. Second, this entry illustrates Trotman's unrelenting desire to build relationships for the gospel. Gurney Harris, Norton, Jowers, Bell, and Johansson were early Navigator leaders who entered The Navs as average, normal Christians. Having no other alternative, they forged relationships built upon the foundation of God and His Word. The result of these relationships was the transformation of five men into leaders for the gospel. Trotman, reflecting on their time together, gloated as a proud spiritual pediatrician over his toddlers in the Lord. They were leading in a discipleship meeting, and we are told that Norton had now assumed a place of leadership in the area of music.

Look back at Trotman's final thoughts on this group of ragtag disciple-makers. These men "dwell together in Unity" because "the Lord has given us such a bond of Love and fellowship." Trotman considered friendships a scarce resource. He knew that they are the only thing we can take to heaven with us and made an intentional effort to enter into friendships for a refined and specific purpose—the advancing of the gospel to all nations. Accordingly, the Lord was the foundation of his relationships and the conversations within them. Trotman did not aspire to relate over pop culture, movie trivia, or sports (although he could talk about each of these three aspects of American cultural life). His goal was specific and his foundation was narrow. He built his relationships upon the Rock of Ages.

This approach to fellowship is a striking contrast from the way that younger evangelicals treat relationships today. This approach is a prophetical call for us to reconsider the way we approach relationships today and a challenge for us to reclaim all that we do as unto the Lord (see Colossians 3:23).

God, help us to see our relationships as scarce resources. They are the only thing we can take with us to heaven. So help us to make the most of them for the gospel.

(DOUG)

39

Secure in God's Love

All that the Father gives me will come to me, and whoever comes to
me I will never cast out. For I have come down from heaven, not to
do my own will but the will of him who sent me. And this is the will
of him who sent me, that I should lose nothing of all that he has
given me, but raise it up on the last day. For this is the will of my
Father, that everyone who looks on the Son and believes in him
should have eternal life, and I will raise him up on the last day.

JOHN 6:37-40

S.T.S. Bible Study (ca. 1941)

"No man can pluck me out of HIS hands. Now, belonging to CHRIST
no man can remove me out of that place which is mine. Yes, I can
get out of fellowship, but no one can sever that relationship.
That very thought drives me to pray for closer fellowship and to
pray that my fellowship may match that blessed relationship."

Dawson Trotman was no theologian, but he had seen enough examples
in his life and ministry of what happens when those who embrace the
gospel do not embrace fellowship with the God of the gospel. The story
of Dawson's picking up a hitchhiker and leading him to Christ and then
a year later picking up the same man and seeing no presence of the new
life in him is foundational to understanding all that Dawson and then
later The Navigators are about. We have a great God, great in mercy and

abounding in love. The gospel is good news. These truths should have a profound impact on our lives. Why was there no difference in the hitchhiker?

The good news is not just about the afterlife; it is good news for the here and now. We can know God, know Him personally. But that relationship does not happen by accident or merely by being a Christian. Daws knew that we have to draw near to God, and in so doing, He draws near to us (see James 4:8). He also knew that while it is God who saves us and brings new life into our beings (see Philippians 2:13), at the same time we have to work and participate in this new life (see Philippians 2:12).

So why do we read the Scriptures? To know God, to know His heart for us and the nation, better. To know of His love, His holiness, His majesty. Why did Daws have people memorizing Scripture? Because he knew that that which we hide in our hearts transforms our hearts and draws us closer to God. Why did he make prayer central to the Christian life? Because fellowship with God comes from talking to and hearing from our beloved Father. Why do we witness? Because it is in sharing the good news of Jesus that we become aware ourselves of how great is our God, how wonderful are His promises. When we share the gospel with others, we have fellowship with the Holy Spirit who is the one true evangelist.

The obedient Christian life is ultimately one that is drawing closer and closer to God at every moment possible. Here is the greatest news: We know that God desires to have fellowship with us all the time. As He said through the apostle Paul, "Rejoice always, pray without ceasing, give thanks in all circumstances; for this is the will of God in Christ Jesus for you. Do not quench the Spirit. Do not despise prophecies, but test everything; hold fast what is good. Abstain from every form of evil" (1 Thessalonians 5:16-22). God is always there for us, always ready for deeper fellowship with us; the question is, are we ready and willing to embrace that fellowship?

Daws also knew that we still fall short of God's glory, that we still sin. But nothing and no one can pluck us from His hand. What a great promise. When we sin (and Daws knew that the young men and women he was working with were not perfect), we cannot listen to our Enemy who tells us to run and hide from God! We belong to God—period! So we must hold firm to that promise and return to the light. The promises of God about being safe and sure in His hand are not permission to avoid deeper fellowship, to avoid the life that God promises. They are the encouragement for us, no matter where we were, no matter how badly we mess up, no matter how far we feel from God, to return to Him, to reenter fellowship with our Savior. God wants to be in fellowship with us, no matter what. The whole of Dawson's life and ministry was about helping himself and others to have that fellowship every day, every hour, in every situation.

I thank You that You have saved me, and that I am safe in Your hand. But I want to know You better. I want to love You more. I want to be the person You made me to be. Help me to grow deeper in You. And help me to grow while I be light in a world that needs to know Your good news. In the name of our Savior, Amen.

(CHRISTOPHER MORTON)

40

The Fellowship of Peace

On the evening of that day, the first day of the week, the doors being locked where the disciples were for fear of the Jews, Jesus came
and stood among them and said to them, "Peace be with you."

JOHN 20:19

S.T.S. Bible Study (ca. 1941)

"V. 19, The mention of the fear of the Jews indicates that this
was a group of believers that met together for fellowship. At
such a time 'came Jesus and stood in the midst, and said unto
them, Peace be unto you' [KJV]. Here was the need of the hour, and
He had the remedy for that. Nothing will take the place of my
getting together with other CHRISTians in fellowship where the
LORD can bless as He promised in Matt. 18:20 and in Malachi 3:16."

After seeing Jesus crucified, the horrified disciples fled to an upper room
and locked themselves in. They had no idea if the mob that called out for
Jesus' death would be coming after them, or if the Roman soldier whose
ear Peter cut off would be coming after revenge. Imagine their shock
when the man they had seen killed and buried suddenly appeared in
their barricaded room. Christ showed them His pierced hands and side
and twice told them, "Peace be with you" (John 20:19,21). As Trotman

noted, their need of the hour was peace and freedom from the extreme terror that had gripped them, and Christ provided that.

There is something powerful about a group of believers meeting together, whether in times of fear or joy. The writer of Hebrews encouraged believers to "consider how to stir up one another to love and good works" (Hebrews 10:24). Historically, Christian fellowship has been an important cornerstone of The Navigators. During World War II, Navigator sailors like Jim Downing and Victor McAnney met together aboard their battleships to study the Word and to witness to their friends. In such perilous times, Christian fellowship strengthened the weary and ushered in the peace of Christ.

As you face tremulous times, nothing can take the place of meeting together with other believers to pray, strengthen each other in the Word, and to preach the peace of Christ to one another. Nothing will take the place of your getting together with fellow Christians in fellowship where the Lord can bless as He promised.

Lord, please place me in a community of fellow Christians where we can strengthen and encourage each other. Please let our hearts burn with godly love for one another and be pleased to meet with us as we seek after You.

(SUSAN)

MAKE DISCIPLES. / John.
                    CHRIST
                    PAUL.

THE NEED......

   95% of the People...
   NEED FOR THE GOSPEL.

THREE FOLD JOB..... { Pioneer
                      EVANGELIZATION.
                      FOLLOW UP.

   CHINA.
      HAS THE BIBLE
      EVANGELIZATION — Honolulu — We Cant

CHAIN AS STRONG AS ITS WEAKEST
                      LINK-----

   JOB ISN'T BEING DONE.
   N. S. E. WEST-

   TALBOT — 12,000-----

   NAVIGATORS -.----
      ALL SCHOOLS- EVERY CITY.
      FIRST SHIP-----

WHAT WE PROPOSE TO DO
SEND PROVEN MEN.
HUBE — NEPAL-
Roy CHINA.

41

One-to-One Discipleship Helps in Spiritual Growth

Paul, an apostle of Christ Jesus by the will of God according to the promise of the life that is in Jesus, to Timothy, my beloved child . . .

2 TIMOTHY 1:1-2

Faithful Men (ca. 1946)

"Every child of GOD is entitled to personal, regular, continued help in HIS CHRISTian life. Why should the Ephesian elders, any more than any other people, have been permitted to have three years of faithful teaching and warning from Paul? Many CHRISTians today cannot point to a single period in their lives when they have had individual help. . . . Their entire knowledge of the Scriptures has come thru the general information given in groups."

One of the most challenging issues in the interpretation and application of Scripture relates to the question of whether a narrative account of a past event is descriptive or prescriptive, whether it informs about "the way things were" or whether it commands "the way things ought to be."

Some Bible events are primarily descriptive, others are primarily prescriptive, and others are a mixture of both.

Exodus 3 relates an encounter between God and Moses that is primarily descriptive in nature. No one else is likely to have a personal "burning bush" experience. On the other hand, the words of Jesus in Matthew 11:28-29 are primarily prescriptive in nature. Coming to Christ when we are weary and burdened is an experience that should be common to all people everywhere. In contrast to each of these, the words of the man born blind, "though I was blind, now I see" (John 9:25) are both descriptive (not everyone will be cured of physical blindness) and prescriptive (everyone should expect to "see" in a new way as a result of being reborn to new life in Christ).

Some people might argue that Paul's relationship with Timothy was descriptive rather than prescriptive, that it merely describes a special situation involving two unique people, and that it should not be expected to be "generalized" to other people in other places and times. Paul regularly referred to Timothy as his "child" and even his "true child" (see 1 Corinthians 4:17; 1 Timothy 1:2,18; 2 Timothy 1:2; 2:1). In this respect, that relationship appears to be unique. However, Paul also referred to Titus (see Titus 1:4) and Onesimus (see Philemon 1:10) using this same type of language. Perhaps Paul's relationship with Timothy was not so unique after all.

Daws had no doubt that the parent/child relationship described between Paul and Timothy was, in every sense, both descriptive and prescriptive. Every Christian, he argued, is not only enriched by such a relationship but is also entitled to it, and in fact even requires it and should demand it. Why, he asked, should some people have the blessing of the fellowship of a true father in the faith while other children are abandoned as spiritual orphans? Anyone who knew Daws or has listened to his messages can recall hearing him cry out, "Men, where is your man? Women, where is your woman?" Here, however, Daws is challenging us with deeper questions. Christians, where are your spiritual children? Are you seeing to their nurture and growth, their care and development, or have you abandoned them for others to raise or to perish alone? Christian children, where are your spiritual parents? Who is giving you care and support, teaching you to walk and to speak, providing the environment in which you grow in maturity before the Enemy can cause you to wither and perish?

There are rare and unfortunate circumstances in human life in which parents, after careful and deliberate thought, and with the best interests of the children in mind, decide to place their children in the care of other people. This situation should be just as rare in the Christian life, but unfortunately this is all too common. Many Christians assume that spiritual parents have fulfilled their entire obligation to their spiritual children by assisting in their birth, and that all of the remainder of their nurture and growth is the responsibility of someone else. As a result, most Christians today "cannot point to a single period in their lives when they have had individual help." Imagine what the overall health of churches today would be if we began to view Paul's relationship with Timothy not only as descriptive of a past event but also as prescriptive for all.

Lord God, why should some Christians be favored with years of the faithful fellowship and care of spiritual parents while so many other Christians are deprived of this blessing? We know the answer to this question, Lord, even as we ask. It should never be so! Strengthen us, Lord, for the task of spiritual parenthood. While much can be learned in classes and in groups, some things can be taught only through direct, personal attention. May we begin to demand always and everywhere that Christians see this once again as both our birthright and our obligation.

(KEN)

42

No Substitute for Time in Teaching People to Follow Christ

And he went up on the mountain and called to him those whom he desired, and they came to him. And he appointed twelve (whom he also named apostles) so that they might be with him.

MARK 3:13-14

Faithful Men (ca. 1946)

"We have since discovered that challenge produces decision, and decision, though important, is but five percent of the job. Ninety-five percent is *working the decision*, which demands that the one challenged be shown ways and means by which he can obey and fulfill the challenge. We had yet to discover that this cannot be accomplished in mass production. In the 'Minute Man' plan, we had made no provision for the type of follow-up which has since proved to be necessary." (emphasis added)

It may sound overly trite and cliché to say, "Jesus is our model" with respect to the methods we employ in making disciples, yet for any Bible-believing Christian, there really is no other place to start than with the example of Jesus. In our contemporary approaches to disciple-making, the key question should be "What *did* Jesus do?" rather than "What *would* Jesus do?"

That Jesus actually *made* disciples is self-evident in Scripture. After all, the people who followed Jesus were called *disciples* throughout the Gospels. It should be equally self-evident that Jesus could have gone about the process of making disciples in a number of different ways. He could have based His ministry in Jerusalem and started a megachurch (mega synagogue, perhaps?) in which masses of people could have come to hear Him teach and preach on a regular basis over many months or even years. He chose not to do it that way. He could have worked within the available structures of the rabbinical schools of His day, working His way up the ladder until He became the dean or the department chair of one of the largest training centers. Again, He chose not to do it that way. In the "fullness of time," God could have waited for the emergence of the technological age so that Jesus could have worked through print, TV, or the Internet. He chose not to do it that way either.

Instead, Jesus chose to work directly through the investment of Himself and His time in the lives of a small number of select individuals. He appointed twelve men, "so that they might be with him," and He poured himself into these specific people. Rather than choosing to work through buildings, programs, or resources, Jesus chose to work through intimate, personal, relational fellowship with just twelve men. Yes, He occasionally preached to larger groups, and yes, He even had at least seventy more people who were also called "disciples," but the corner-stone of His ministry was His close, intentional fellowship with the core group of men who were called simply "the Twelve" or "the disciples."

In the final years of his ministry, as Daws was looking back over all of the methods he had employed and as he was attempting to describe in explicit detail the Navigator way of making disciples, he noted that

5 percent of the task was getting people to make the commitment, and 95 percent of the task was holding them to that commitment. "Working the decision" to Daws meant making the investment of personal time and effort in the lives of new believers, and taking personal responsibility for guiding them in the process of growth toward spiritual maturity. The *tools* The Navigators used were simple, and they could easily be mass-produced, but the *application* of the tools to the individual failed miserably in a mass-production environment. The "type of follow-up which [eventually] proved to be necessary" required a resource that cannot be mass-produced: fellowship.

Lord God, the principle of disciple-making through fellowship seems simple, but only You fully realize how difficult and demanding it is. After all, it cost You everything You had to give just to bring it into being. The ease of mass production is alluring, Lord, for we live in an age in which the idols of "more," "fast," and "efficient" have their altars in almost every home. Help us, we pray, to see with fresh eyes that the slower method of discipleship through fellowship was Your preferred method, and may we yield graciously and willingly to the greater demands that this method places on our lives and on our time.

(KEN)

Witnessing

43

The Witness of a Transformed Life

But now that you have been set free from sin and have become slaves of God, the fruit you get leads to sanctification and its end, eternal life.

ROMANS 6:22

AlphAmegA Bible Study (ca. 1942)

"There is no doubt about the fact that the most convincing sermon is a transformed life, one dead to sin, freed from it, raised to newness of life, has all the power of demonstrating to an unbelieving world the absolute total change to be presenting this convincing argument. By GOD'S grace, I must show for the fruits of a holy life and 'gain a hearing' for those who up to this time have never been freed from sin and know they are in bondage to it."

Daws certainly knew a thing or two about a transformed life. After graduating from high school, he began drinking and gambling, and spent some time in jail after he was too drunk to find his car one night. One afternoon, he and a girlfriend tried to swim across a lake. The distance was greater than either one of them had anticipated and they began to flounder. Fearing they would both drown, Dawson cried out to the Lord, telling

Him, "If You save us, I'll do whatever You want me to!" The Lord did rescue them that day and Dawson began going back to church. After Dawson memorized Scripture for a Sunday school contest in order to impress a girl, the Word began having an impact in his life. One day when he was on his way to work at the lumberyard, John 1:12-13 flashed into his mind and he realized what salvation means.

When he surrendered to Christ, his life changed dramatically. The man who had spent his time racing around town on his motorcycle and drinking now spent time telling others about Jesus. The sailors whom he would eventually minister to could relate to the rough-and-tumble Dawson and seeing how much his life had changed in Christ made a huge impact on them.

As you seek to reach people for Christ, demonstrate the fruits of a holy life and gain a hearing from the people around you. Your redeemed life has the power to lead people in bondage to sin to the One who can save them to the uttermost.

Lord, thank You for setting me free from sin and for sanctifying me. Please work in my life to produce good fruit and use my testimony to lead others to Yourself.

(SUSAN)

WORLD VISION

GOD LOVED The WORLD. "they've been robbed"
ABRAM - Key Person. { Jews The Bible
                   { Seed - CHRIST
    ALL FAMILIES - - - - - - - - { a family starts
                                    with one seed

JOHN 17:18   Gospel seed from
                              a foreign Country

People ask where will ye labor.   Can't keep bring-
     Sent to the WORLD.   ing seed.
TRUE VISION Not Just A Field. (pray for me)

WHAT THE WORD TEACHES

I   A   WHO
          HEATHEN - - - -   Psa 96:3
          GENTILES - - -   ISA 60:11
          ALL NATIONS -   ROM 16:26

   B.   WHERE END of EARTH - -   Acts 13:47
              EARTH FILLED - -   ISA 11:9

Wait   ⌈ HOW   Bud, SEED,   Isa 61:11 ⌉
      ⌊ and when ⌋

   C. WHAT.   Righteousness ⎫ - -   Isa 61:11
               Obededience ⎭   Psa 18:44

II   HOW.
     a. Ask   Psa 2:8 - (John
     b   GO - - { MK 16:15
              { sent John 17:18
     c. MAKE DISCIPLES
       1. Bud seed.   Isa 61:11
       2. 0-0-0-0   Acts 1:8.

44

Going All-Out for the Gospel

For unto whomsoever much is given, of him shall be much required.

LUKE 12:48 (KJV)

"America's Responsibility in the Post-War World," in *Christ's Ambassadors*, December 1944

"Now, here is where we come in. The job of world evangelization is to be done by individuals. God has always done His greatest work through a man. The Lord will use us if we are willing. Oh Christian, what is our obligation? It is to go all-out for the Lord Jesus by helping to deliver the peoples of the world from the clutches of the deadly enemy of souls (Isa. 61:1)."

In December 1944 Dawson Trotman anticipated the end of the Second World War and looked ahead to the future. American politicians began to prepare for rebuilding war-ravaged Europe and Japan. Similarly, American Christians prepared for the healing of souls and the spread of the gospel into lands stricken of hope.

The war years galvanized The Navigators into a sold-out generation of young men and women ministering aboard ships all over the Pacific, in homes, and hospitals. The magazine *Christ's Ambassadors* called The Navigators "that wide-awake generation of Christian servicemen who are always busy with their Bibles." Now at the end of the war, The Navigators faced a new challenge. In this article for the magazine, Trotman urged Christians to "go all-out for the Lord Jesus by helping to deliver the peoples of the world from the clutches of the deadly enemy of souls."

Daws asserted that American Christians had three responsibilities: First, American Christians were to get missionaries ready. Trotman encouraged Christians to lead as many young men and women to Christ as possible and to disciple them. He urged young believers to start preparing for missionary service by attending Bible school and seminary and learning foreign languages.

Second, Trotman outlined the importance of sending missionaries. During the war, travel restrictions had severely limited the freedom that missionaries had to leave the United States and enter war-torn countries. In late 1944, however, Trotman anticipated a time when hostilities would cease and people would be free to go wherever the Lord sent them. Daws embraced new forms of transportation and encouraged missionary organizations to "provide up-to-date and adequate means of transportation by use of airplane, helicopter, etc. If the gospel is the greatest thing in all the world, it is worthy of the greatest investment."

Finally, he encouraged Christians to support missionaries on the field. Daws asked American believers to pray for laborers among the harvest, to write letters of encouragement, and to send material aid. "Our nation is not *tithing* its money in its war effort," he wrote. "Rather, ninety per cent of what we are spending now is going into this all-out effort to deliver the nations of the world from the clutches of a terrible God-hating foe."

Surely Christians have the obligation to go all-out to rescue people from the deadly Enemy of their souls. In our own era, we must continue to prepare missionaries for service. We must use whatever new means of transportation and technology are available to us to cross into the Enemy's territory to bring light and hope. We must use our resources to go all-out in the effort to rescue the nations from the clutches of the deadly Enemy of their souls.

Lord, please help me go all-out for Christ by rescuing the people of the world from the clutches of the deadly Enemy of their souls. Give us wisdom on how to prepare for the harvest and how to use new forms of transportation and technology. Please grant us passage to countries closed to the gospel. Give us wisdom in how to use our resources that You've given us in an all-out manner for You.

(SUSAN)

45

The Lord's Messenger in the Lord's Message

Now the eleven disciples went to Galilee, to the mountain to which Jesus had directed them. And when they saw him they worshiped him, but some doubted. And Jesus came and said to them, "All authority in heaven and on earth has been given to me. Go therefore and make disciples of all nations, baptizing them in the name of the Father and of the Son and of the Holy Spirit, teaching them to observe all that I have commanded you. And behold, I am with you always, to the end of the age."

MATTHEW 28:16-20

Faithful Men (ca. 1946)

"The question will be asked, 'What do we mean by men of GOD, holy men, bondservants, real soldiers, obedient sons?' We mean men who are the embodiment of the message they carry, men who have a knowledge of the Word of GOD, and who lay hold of the promises of GOD, who are obedient to the will of GOD, and who then carry the message of GOD, men of whom it may be said, as was said of Haggai, that they are the LORD's messenger in the LORD's message (Haggai 1:13)."

In the evangelical church traditions of North America, the Great Commission gets much attention in both word and deed. The church

170

spends multiplied tens of millions of dollars on gospel work, but most studies would indicate that born-again followers of Jesus Christ make up a smaller percentage of the population today than they did a decade ago, or a decade before that, or a decade before that. With all of the money and attention placed on fulfilling the Great Commission, why do our efforts often seem so lacking in fruit?

One part of the reason could be that in our interpretation of the Great Commission we focus too much of our attention on the word "go," and too little on the words "make disciples" and "teaching them to observe all that I have commanded you." Another part of the reason could be that we depend too much on programs and people and too little on the One who holds "all authority in heaven and on earth" to empower all of our programs and people.

On the surface, these few verses from Matthew's gospel seem disarmingly simple. The disciples were to go and multiply themselves, making more disciples. As they had been taught, they were to teach others. In the power and authority of Jesus, and in the full assurance of His continuing presence, they were to obey His command to be used of God in bringing more people into the body of Christ. What could be simpler?

During the final years of his life, Daws was working on a book that was intended to offer a full expression of his theology and practice in the work of The Navigators. For nearly three decades, he had been maturing in his understanding that people only begin the process of becoming "men of God" when they first respond to the call of the gospel. To those who believe in the name of Jesus, God grants the right to become *children* of God, but *men* of God take time to produce.

For Daws, the messenger and the message were tied closely together. Evangelism was a constant activity for Daws, but it was never a program. It was the communication of the *gift* of life and it was the *way* of life. It rested upon the communication of a clear message of salvation, but it was never reduced to just the sharing of that message.

Daws was amazed to discover early in his Christian life that even a "baby" in Christ can effectively share the message of salvation. In an

S.T.S. Bible study on John 4:35 in October 1940, Daws wrote of "[the] thrill of knowing that I can immediately plunge into the work and win souls even while I am learning how." However, he grew to appreciate that the most effective evangelism takes place when the people who are sharing the message of the life-changing power of the name of Jesus demonstrate the power of that message in their own lives.

The Great Commission gives a simple command: people who are disciples are to obey God by helping to create new disciples. For Daws, the people who carry the message must themselves *be* the message. He spent most of his life helping the church relearn how to turn message-carriers into message-bearers. Are we forgetting this once again in our day, and could this be why our evangelism often bears so little fruit?

Lord God, help those of us who carry Your message of saving grace to embody the power and blessing of this message. May we be and become disciples who place ourselves under the teaching and cleansing of Your Word, that we may lay hold anew of Your promises of power and authority and presence, and that we may be rekindled in our passion to be Your messengers in the message.

(KEN)

BEATENBERG   AUG 15 '48

THE NEED OF THE HOUR.

NOT ---- MORE BLDGS OR GREATER
         MORE OR NEW & NOVEL METHODS
         NOT MORE BOOKS ABOUT THE BIBLE

         NOT ALONE MORE MEETINGS.

    MEN - MIGHTY MEN —
              OF FAITH
CALIFORNIA --- MEN TO MATCH MY MOUNTAINS.

    PARADOX- WHAT IS MAN ----   OTHER HAND.
              I WILL WORK. ----   SEE THE GREAT
                                              GOD.
                    }   ISA 59:16 51:18 64:7

         WATCH THE MAN MOSES.
            WATCH ISREAL- DID EVIL
                           DID RIGHT

    The SCARLET THREAD
         GOLDEN   "
      " HUMAN   " — II Pet 2:21 ——
    THE TRAGEDY-- ARE THE FEW (HEB. 11)   ELIJAH
                                          The 7000

    SOMEONE   GOD HAS YET.
      The WEAKNESS. — ONLY of Self —
    TRUE ?-- I COR 1:27   I Sam 16:7
              Psa 8:2.

II JOHN 8-2.
    MY LITTLE CHILDREN— until CHRIST BE FORMED

              FOLLOW UP.
    NIGHT AND DAY- — might perfect that which is lack.
    IN ANY PROVIDE
    WHAT HAVE YOU TO LAY AT HIS FEET
      ONE SINNER DESTROYETH—
      BY This — Great Cause.

    TWINS.

46

The "Need of the Hour" Is Still People Who Are Sold Out for the Work of Christ

And I heard the voice of the Lord saying, "Whom shall I send, and who will go for us?" Then I said, "Here am I! Send me."

ISAIAH 6:8

Faithful Men (ca. 1946)

"And down through the ages we feel that the cry of GOD is for men that HE could use. Some of the most tragic verses of all the Bible are simply the account of God's looking and failure to be able to find a man of the hour for the need of the Hour. 'And there is none that calleth upon THY Name, that stirreth up himself to take hold of thee . . .' (Isa 64:7 [KJV]). 'And HE saw that there was no man, and wondered that there was no intercessor' (Isa 59:16 [KJV]). 'And I sought for a man among them, that should make up the hedge, and stand in the gap before ME for the land, that I should not destroy it: but I found none' (Ezek 22:30 [KJV]). GOD's

quest for men that HE could trust and men that HE could use is
beautifully portrayed in the statement '. . . I have found David
the son of Jesse, a man after MINE own heart, which shall fulfill
all my will' (Acts 13:22 [KJV]). It has been the thing for which
HE has sought from the beginning."

Isaiah saw three things that made him ready and willing to commit his
life fully to God's service. First, he saw God as God wished to be seen. All
people have an idea of what God might be like, but "the hour is coming,
and is now here, when the true worshipers will worship the Father in
spirit and truth" (John 4:23). Isaiah saw God revealed in all of His *true*
majesty, holiness, and glory. Just as Job once said, "I had heard of you by
the hearing of the ear, but now my eye sees you" (Job 42:5), Isaiah
actually saw God exalted above all creation, sovereign over all creation,
and worthy of worship by all creation.

Second, Isaiah saw himself. In the light of God's infinite glory, he
saw his own sinfulness, brokenness, lostness, and helplessness. He knew
that he was "undone," and he knew that the only thing he could do was
to cry out to God in his recognition of the miserable condition to which
he had brought himself.

Third, he saw that worship of God results in service to God. The
seraphim worshipped God by serving Him. Isaiah knew in an instant
that God had in sovereignty created him, had in sovereignty redeemed
him, and had a right in sovereignty to direct him. As Mary would later
say, "Behold, I am the servant of the Lord; let it be to me according to
your word" (Luke 1:38), Isaiah would now say, "Let your desire be as a
command to me."

Daws yearned to be a willing and fitting servant of the Lord. He was
ready to go anywhere and do anything at the command and will of God.
Even more than that, however, he yearned for God to use him in helping
to find and train other people for the same readiness to worship God
through the service of their lives. Daws grieved that so few people were
ready and willing to "get down to business" and totally consecrate

themselves to the Lord's service, but he refused to be paralyzed by his grief. He knew with an absolute certainty that God was always looking for someone to send and that in every generation people were ready to rise to "the need of the hour" and go to any length in God's service. It was one of the joys of Daws' life to be used of God to help people catch Isaiah's vision and say, "Here am I! Send me."

Lord God, here am I. Send me! Send me anywhere, Lord, so long as You send me to serve You. Send me to anyone, Lord, that You may use me to bring them into Your service. Send me at any time, Lord, that I may help bring people to awareness that "the need of the hour" remains unchanged and that You still desire people who will worship You by serving You with the fullness of their lives. Send me, Lord, and in sending me, may You spend me in your work of finding and equipping others who will be sent and spent in service to You!

(KEN)

47

No Matter the Means, the Main Thing Is Still Discipleship

As we pray most earnestly night and day that we may see you face to face and supply what is lacking in your faith.

1 THESSALONIANS 3:10

Faithful Men (ca. 1946)

"Church history today is not what GOD did thru a denomination. It is the result, in most cases, of what he did thru the man Luther, the man Calvin, the man Wesley, the man Moody. Modern missions are not the result of mass movements, but of what HE could do thru men such as Livingston, Morrison, Carey, Taylor, Mary Slessor and Judson. . . . Is GOD going to change HIS plan in reaching the World today? Will it be the radio, the printing press, the airplane which will do the job? These will all play their part, but the need of the hour is for men—and not just one man. The lateness of the hour, the tremendous size of the task, calls for men, holy men of GOD, strong, rugged soldiers of the Cross with an eye single to HIS Glory, men that will hazard their lives for the Name of the LORD JESUS, men who will bring their bodies into subjection, men of prayer, intercessors, men who, like Paul, could say 'Night and day praying exceedingly that we might see your face, and might perfect that which is lacking in your faith' (1 Thess 3:10 [KJV]), men who will not only preach the word in season, and out of season, but will, as Paul did, stick with those they preach to three months, six months, a year and a half, two years, three years, men who will go back over the hazardous journeys and follow up their converts as he did whether by foot or sailing vessels, thru storms, with or without companions."

If Dawson Trotman were alive today, I think he would find the modern evangelistic training programs, methods, and strategies to be tiresome exercises — not because he would be against evangelism or strategies, but because he would find them to be overly complicated and convoluted. Now for the record, there was no bigger proponent of evangelism in the early twentieth century than Dawson Earle Trotman. This was a man who was known to intimidate people upon first meeting because he generally began his introductions by saying, "Hi, I am Daws Trotman. What Scripture verse are you memorizing today?" This is the same man who once chided Billy Graham for not being theological enough in his mass-evangelism strategies. This is the same man who told an eager and teachable sailor that he would not train him in discipleship because the sailor was not willing to give his right arm for the gospel.

These strategies often provide an intellectual excuse to hide from a heart problem. Often times these strategies and programs subtly communicate that some form of intellectual training and logical reasoning is a prerequisite for *true* evangelism. Thus, people who may be apprehensive in sharing the gospel (the heart issue) often seek refuge in training programs or strategies as a way to avoid having to put the gospel into daily practice. It is for that reason that Trotman would be uninterested in modern evangelism strategies.

Toward the end of his life, Dawson Trotman gave a series of speeches that constituted the seasoned reflections of a wise and experienced evangelist. These classic speeches *Born to Reproduce, The Need of the Hour,* and *Power to Re-Create* offered Trotman the forum to mobilize the often-immobile Christian body of his time. In his unfinished manuscript *Faithful Men,* Trotman picks up on his main theme of "the need of the hour" suggesting that the "main" need is not further *training,* but further *doing* of the gospel.

Though Trotman was uneasy about denominational affiliation, his criticism of denominations in this section is not meant to be disparaging. By contrast, Trotman is prophetically reminding men and women to understand that God's plan for saving the world remains the same as it did in Paul and Luther's day—we are to be about leading people to Christ and then teaching them to lead other people to Christ.

Media such as radio, printing, and television are just that—*means* for aiding the main thing, which is evangelism and discipleship. Denominations too are *means* to the end. They help in the mass organization and execution of the main thing of evangelism and discipleship. Trotman was saying that when we spend too great a time discussing whether radio or printing is a better means of mass communication, or whether we should coordinate with Baptist or Methodist churches, we tend to lose sight of the main thing. Those things are good means. But Trotman reminds us that means do not change our central focus and task at hand—evangelism and discipleship.

God, help us to make the main thing our main thing. And would You continue to make disciples by whatever means You desire. Continue to use the church to reproduce the church, for Your glory and for our good.

(DOUG)

48

A Passion for Individuals

He said to them, "Go into all the world and proclaim the gospel to the whole creation."

MARK 16:15

**Letter to Jim and Velma Kiefer,
Frankfurt, Germany, September 28, 1949**

"I am not interested in filling up the time in Europe with large meetings but rather I am trusting Him to lead me to certain individuals with whom time may be spent on this matter of getting individual CHRIST-ians into the Word in order to grow and be able to propagate the Word individually by multiplication. I trust you will pray with me regarding this."

In 1949 Dawson Trotman received a call to preach the gospel in Europe. Daws had returned from a trip to China only a few months before the country fell to communism, and he felt keenly the urgency of the world political situation. In an era when totalitarian governments were gaining strangleholds over many nations, Trotman wanted to spread the gospel to as many places as possible before they became closed off. He also saw the need to minister to souls ravaged during World War II. In this letter to Jim and Velma Kiefer of Frankfurt,

Germany, he explained his vision for Europe.

The concept of spiritual multiplication and discipleship of individual believers interested Daws. Although he would later partner with Billy Graham during his London crusade in 1955, Trotman's heart remained focused on the individual Christian. He desired to follow up believers who had made decisions at large crusades, helping them read and memorize Scripture. In turn, he wanted these Christians to take someone else under their wing and teach them how to do the same thing—spiritual multiplication. To Dawson, the fulfillment of the Great Commission was each person telling another person about Christ and teaching them to obey their Savior in all things. Late in World War II, Daws coined a term for this concept: reproducing reproducers.

This method was counterintuitive to missiology of the day. Instead of large meetings and tent revivals, Daws focused on individual hearts that yearned to grow in faith. Christ doesn't need stadiums full of people or a dynamic speaker. He is simply looking for individuals who are willing to dig into His Word and share it with others.

Lord, please lead to me Christians who are interested in soaking up the Word in order to grow. I pray especially for the individual Christians living under totalitarian regimes, in war-ravaged countries, and in places closed politically and spiritually to the gospel.

(SUSAN)

49

Reproducing Disciples "According to Their Kind"

And God said, "Let the earth sprout vegetation, plants yielding seed, and fruit trees bearing fruit in which is their seed, each according to its kind, on the earth." And it was so. The earth brought forth vegetation, plants yielding seed according to their own kinds, and trees bearing fruit in which is their seed, each according to its kind. And God saw that it was good. . . . And God blessed them. And God said to them, "Be fruitful and multiply."

GENESIS 1:11-12,28

Power to Re-Create (ca. 1953)

"Effective follow-up begins with effective evangelism. It includes providing conditions for a healthy spiritual birth, digestible food for the spiritual infant, and protection from spiritual disease. Training and correction, encouragement and challenge, instruction and example all contribute toward the goal expressed by the Apostle Paul: 'Till we all come in the unity of the faith, and of the knowledge of the Son of God, unto a perfect man, unto the measure of the stature of the fullness of Christ' (Ephesians 4:13 [KJV])."

When God created the world, He made each kind of living thing unique from every other kind of living thing. Oak trees were a different kind of living thing than blue whales, and they were even a different kind of living thing than apple trees (or maple trees, or any other kind of trees). Not only was each kind of living thing created unique in itself, each kind of living thing was created able to reproduce according to its kind and *only* according to its kind. Oak trees were not created able to bring forth blue whales or apples, apple trees were not created able to bring forth acorns or whales, and whales were not created able to bring forth acorns or apples. Each living thing was to "be fruitful and multiply" after its own kind.

In *Born to Reproduce*, Daws observes from the first chapter of Genesis, "The first order ever given to man was that he 'be fruitful and multiply.' In other words, he was to reproduce after his own kind. God did not tell Adam and Eve, our first parents, to be spiritual. They were already in His image. Sin had not yet come in. He just said, 'Multiply. I want more just like you, more in my own image.'" However, Daws also made a spiritual connection to the physical reality expressed in the Genesis account. He noted, "In the physical realm when your children have children, you become a grandparent. Your parents are then great-grandparents, and theirs are great-great-grandparents. *And so it should be in the spiritual.*"

In *Power to Re-Create*, Daws draws our attention to the fact that spiritual reproduction lies at the very heart of the Great Commission. The point of evangelism is not just to create "converts," and the point of disciple-making is not just to create people capable of "doing evangelism." According to Daws, evangelism that results in people who are incapable of reproducing after their own kind is *ineffective* evangelism, and follow-up that results in people who are incapable of reproducing after their own kind is ineffective follow-up.

Daws was adamant on this point. Effective follow-up begins with effective evangelism, and at the same time, effective evangelism begins with effective follow-up. The goal is that we "all come in the unity of the faith" to mature manhood in Christ, to the place where we are spiritually mature enough to reproduce more people of the same kind who are themselves spiritually mature reproducers according to their kind. As Daws states, this process takes "training and correction, encouragement and challenge, instruction and example." In other words, it takes effort, intentionality, equipping, and time.

According to Daws, effective evangelism takes place in an environment where nurture and growth are planned in advance and capable of taking place. It has as its goal not just the sharing of a message, and not just the urgent appeal for a response, but also the desire to see spiritual "generations" of believers reproducing after their own kind.

Lord God, as children born anew to a living faith, created in Your image and likeness, created in Christ Jesus for the good works You purposed for us to do, renew in us a vision for reproducing after our own kind, which is to say, after Your kind. Help us, we pray, to be effective in our follow-up by being effective in our evangelism, and help us to be effective in our evangelism by being effective in our follow-up. May we never slip into the easy complacency of thinking that we can do one without doing the other.

(KEN)

Y.F.C.
MEDICINE LAKE  WHICH FIRST
chick Egg.
child parent.

GOAL { 1. OUR GOAL? ---- MUST BE HIS GOAL
WHAT DOES HE WANT
>< GO BACK TO THE BOOK ><

CONSIDER.

THEY MUST BE WON ⊃≡ ISA 53:-10,11
II Pet 3:9

1   Peter { Acts 2:38- Repent
Acts 3:19 Repent, Be Converted..

2.   Paul { Acts 16:31- Believe

⟨WATCH⟩ PETER AND PAUL KNEW FOLLOW UP.
I Peter - Read { 1:18 --- Follow 1:14, 22 etc
2: 24 --- 2:9   2:20 etc
3: 18 ---- 3:15 3:12 .. also 4' 5'

II Pet (Likewise) Espec. II Pet 1:12,
1: 8, 9

≪ { NOTE II Pet 3:9- (3:10 3:14 etc) ≫ 4.

PAUL
Acts 16:31 - also 16:32 (stayed all night)
ISAIAH 53----

1. THE REVIVAL
AT PENTECOST } ---- Preceded --- { †
Note why   Life
Miracles
Death
Resurrection
Prayer (days)
Holy Spirit
Tongues
Preaching.

2. STEPHEN---- { As great
Think of The   a message
Preparation.   as Peters } -- ONE Man Comes Thru
note

3. PAULS Sermons { mostly Heathen   { 3mo -- Acts 19:8
Saved   { good while -- " 18:18
Followed up -----

50

Follow-Up Is Spiritual Pediatrics

And what you have heard from me in the presence of many witnesses entrust to faithful men who will be able to teach others also.

2 TIMOTHY 2:2

Power to Re-Create (ca. 1953)

"Follow-up is, in effect, spiritual pediatrics."

Toward the end of his life, Dawson Trotman was considered the most knowledgeable expert on the theology and practice of discipleship ministry. Accordingly, Trotman was able to capitalize on his vast experience and history with the discipleship movement by converting his wisdom into several seminal speeches about the particulars of discipleship ministry. These speeches included such famous titles as *Born to Reproduce*, *The Need of the Hour*, and *Power to Re-Create*.

In *Power to Re-Create*, Trotman summarized the whole of discipleship ministry in one key sentence: "Follow-up is, in effect, spiritual pediatrics." This was a significant choice in phrasing because it speaks to three key aspects of discipleship. First, discipleship involves "follow-up." In John 3:3 Jesus said, "Unless one is born again he cannot see the kingdom of God." By the end of the nineteenth century many people believed that being "born again" was the totality of the Christian experience.

Trotman asked a new question: "What happens after conversion?" Accordingly, he taught that mature Christians had a responsibility to "follow up" with those who were converted to make sure that they grew in the Christian faith.

This idea leads to the second aspect—pediatrics. Pediatrics is the branch of medicine that deals with the medical care of infants, children, and adolescents. Trotman understood a basic truism of the Christian experience—Christians exist along a wide spectrum of maturity. There are immature Christians, maturing Christians, and mature Christians. Thus, Trotman saw "follow-up" as consisting of a mature Christian acting as the pediatrician who helps the infant, children, and adolescent Christian to mature in the Christian life.

Finally, discipleship is a *spiritual* process. It is not purely a mental process whereby a mature Christian teaches an immature Christian to memorize a set of biblical principles. It is not purely an emotional process whereby a mature Christian helps a younger Christian to experience the reality of God's presence. It is primarily a spiritual process whereby we learn to love God with heart, mind, soul, and strength.

God, would You raise up maturing Christians who catch the vision for the discipleship process? Teach the church to become an organization of spiritual pediatricians who make follow-up the beat of their collective heart. And would You advance Your kingdom through the entrusting of biblical truth to faithful men and women?

(DOUG)

51

Discipleship Leads to Evangelism

And you became imitators of us and of the Lord, for you received the word in much affliction, with the joy of the Holy Spirit, so that you became an example to all the believers in Macedonia and in Achaia. For not only has the word of the Lord sounded forth from you in Macedonia and Achaia, but your faith in God has gone forth everywhere, so that we need not say anything.

1 THESSALONIANS 1:6-8

"Discipleship," in *Park Street Spire*, June 1956

"Herein lies a tragedy. We lead a soul to Christ, and because that soul is not followed up and taught, his potential is lost. He is sterile. And all the seed that might have come to him is lost."

One of the greatest compliments we give to Christians in contemporary evangelical circles is to bestow upon them the title of "soul winner." How many times have we heard someone introduced this way: "Mr. X has been a pastor for twenty years, is a devoted husband and father, is the author of several books, and is a well-known preacher and speaker, but even more than that, *he is a soul winner!*" Let me be absolutely clear here: I sincerely believe that being used of God to help win souls to Christ is the most important, most exciting, and most rewarding thing that any Christian can ever do, but look closely at 1 Thessalonians 1:6-8. Do you notice anything interesting about it?

These verses mention several attributes and characteristics of the members of the body of Christ in Thessalonica. They were imitators of both Paul and Jesus, they received the word of God (even in much affliction), they were filled with the joy of the Holy Spirit, they became an example to believers in other places, and not only had the word of the Lord gone forth from them into neighboring regions, but their faith had also become widely known. Did you catch it? If "the word of the Lord sounded forth" means that the gospel was proclaimed through them and by them, this characteristic is *not* the "crown jewel" of their résumés. In fact, it is mentioned in a matter-of-fact way, almost as if such should be *expected* rather than *exceptional*. In the rhetorical formula, "not only X but also Y," it is whatever is mentioned *second* that is being emphasized. Here, not only were they evangelistic (the "ordinary" attribute), but more than that their *faith in God had become widely known* (the "extraordinary" attribute worthy of special notice).

In a short church magazine article titled simply *Discipleship*, published in the same month he died, Daws reflected with honesty and humility on one of the key mistakes he had made earlier in his ministry years. He noted that the Minute Men had been busy being "soul winners" but that this had proved, over time, to be an ineffective strategy for reaching multitudes of people with the gospel. In fact, he described their effort as a "tragedy" rather than an accolade!

In a personal journal entry from November 29, 1946, Daws wrote, "There are probably some who feel that the Navigators follow-up, as far as the Christian is concerned, eliminates a good deal of the evangelistic effort. This is not necessarily true because the men with whom we labor actually do more by way of evangelism than we could ever do and their training as a result of our work finds adequate returns [in] the results through their lives." Daws never became complacent about actually *doing* evangelism, but he also recognized that he could do far more evangelism through other people than he could ever do by himself. At some future event, I would love to hear someone introduced *this* way: "Not only is X a soul winner, but he is an equipper and trainer of soul winners who are themselves equippers and trainers of soul winners!"

Lord God, the prayer of our hearts is that we might be used of You and by You to bring other people into a relationship of saving faith with You through the person and work of Your Son, Jesus Christ. We delight each time we have some role to play in proclaiming the good news of the gospel of Your grace. Keep us mindful, Lord, that each person we help lead to faith in You has the potential to multiply the spread of the gospel, and that by ourselves we can never personally reach the multitudes of people who might eventually come to know You. May we serve as examples in this, for all the world to see, for the praise and glory of Your name.

(KEN)

"Super-Christians"

You will be my witnesses in Jerusalem and in all Judea and Samaria,
and to the end of the earth.

ACTS 1:8

NavLog #76, April 1959

"All over the world, men and women are reaching their neighbors
for Christ. They are not 'Super-Christians,' but simply those
who have believed the Gospel, learned how to feed themselves on
the Word of God, and been encouraged to pass it on to someone
else. Some of us have gotten no further than 'Jerusalem' with
our witness (Acts 1:8). Some have not even witnessed at home.
May God help us feed our own soul daily with the Word, live it
before others as we speak it with the authority of God's messengers ... and then train our 'babes' in Christ to follow Him!"

The job of reaching the world for Christ does not belong to the promi-
nent "Super-Christians" of the world. It doesn't belong to Billy Graham
or John Piper or the pastor of your church. It belongs to you. As Dawson
Trotman pointed out in this posthumous article in the April 1959
NavLog, the most effective witness for Christ comes from the everyday
man or woman who believes the gospel and who knows the Word. You
don't have to earn a seminary degree to share the good news. You just
need faith in your Redeemer and grounding in His Word.

Witnessing occurs most naturally through relational networks. The people who already know you are much more likely to listen to your witness than to that of a stranger. Your best friend has much more trust in you and the veracity of your faith than she does in the blockbuster Christian author. Your sister and father have more trust in you than they do in Christian leaders like Franklin Graham. Witnessing at home, in our own Jerusalem, is vital. This passage sums up Daws' method of "reproducing reproducers." Learn the Word and then pass along everything that you know.

Have you thought about going overseas on a mission trip? Witness to your loved ones and neighbors first. May God help nourish our souls with the Word and enable us to pass along the good news to those around us.

Lord, please nourish me with Your Word and let it transform my life. Please use me to let the good news of Your kingdom go forth in my household, my neighborhood, my city, and to the ends of the earth.

(SUSAN)

Classic Daws: Dawson Trotman's Articles and Sermons

Making Your Witness Count

Published in the Far Eastern Gospel Crusader Spring 1953

One sailor lad who came to our Navigators Home in San Pedro some twenty years ago was Jim Downing, a shrewd, skeptical youngster determined to resist the gospel. But he couldn't resist too long the power in the lives of his shipmates on the *West Virginia*—a power that warmed and opened his heart to the Word of God, until one morning alone in a turret on the ship he quietly committed his life to Jesus Christ.

Jim has been leading men to Christ ever since. He soon found to be true something he learned from the men who brought him to the Saviour and from the Book they studied—that leading a man to Christ is only a small part of the job. A man with heart prepared by the Spirit could make his decision for Christ in moments, but it was what went before and the months of patient work that followed that came to count.

What went before? The Apostle Paul had described it in 1 Thessalonians 1:5: "For our gospel came not unto you in word only, but also in power, and in the Holy Ghost, and in much assurance; *as ye know what manner of men we were among you for your sake*" [KJV, emphasis added]. Jim did his daily work aboard ship without complaining and did it well, while non-Christians watched critically for a chink in his character. His unselfish acts and unswerving integrity added weight to the tactful word of witness that he gave. Alone on watch, Jim quietly prayed for his buddies . . . by name.

When the right time came the actual giving of the gospel was simple. Jim usually gave a man a series of questions about the familiar John 3:16 to think over and to answer. Often, a fellow made his decision for Christ alone, as Jim had done.

Through the good seed of the Word dropped into a prepared heart, God performed the miracle of the new birth, bringing another son into His family. Instead of Jim's responsibility ending at this point, it increased. God had placed in his charge a youngster to train — he must begin to teach him how to feed on the Word, to pray, to live a Christ-centered life that would draw other men to the Saviour.

Christ planned that the work of guiding the life of a young believer to maturity and fruitfulness as a disciple should be yours and mine. I am confident this is what He had in mind when He said, "Ye have not chosen me, but I have chosen you, and ordained you, that ye should go and bring forth fruit, *and that your fruit should remain*" (John 15:16, KJV, emphasis added). How else could He have left in the hands of less than a dozen men the task of carrying the gospel to all the world? The order was to go and make disciples of all nations . . . "*teaching them to observe all things whatsoever I have commanded you*" (Matthew 28:20, KJV, emphasis added). Impossible? No — if we apply the "how" as well as the "what" of His command.

Paul did it . . . though a tireless preacher of the gospel, ever traveling to touch new territory with the wonderful news, he constantly took time to train his Timothy . . . Titus . . . or Epaphras of Colosse . . . or Sopater of Berea . . . or others . . . who were to perpetuate and multiply his ministry in future years. This cost him time and effort, even as it had cost Jesus when He withdrew once and again from the multitudes in order to train His men in things needful for the future. There was no shortcut to making disciples.

The Thessalonian Christians reached the world in their generation (see 1 Thessalonians 1:8), and I believe with all my heart that it can be done today, if we follow His order not only to evangelize but to make disciples . . . training them to reach others . . . who will reach others and in turn guide them to spiritual maturity and reproduction (Psalm 78:5-6).

What worked for Thessalonica won't work today, some will say. But it *is* working—in Formosa, for example, where close to 50,000 young converts are studying the Bible individually and winning their neighbors to Christ. They are not "super Christians," but simply those who have believed the gospel and been taught how to feed themselves on the Word of God and then encouraged to pass it on to someone else. We are moving ahead on the simple principle that these babes in Christ can become the disciples that the Thessalonians were, if they are only given some of the parental care required to "disciple" them. Paul referred to this when he wrote, "Ye know how we exhorted and comforted and charged every one of you, as a father doth his children, that ye would walk worthy of God, Who hath called you unto His kingdom and glory" (1 Thessalonians 2:11-12, KJV).

And it worked for Jim Downing. Because he has been faithful in making disciples of the men he has led to Christ, he is an example of those who are beginning to fulfill our Lord's command to be His witnesses "*both* in Jerusalem *and* in all Judea, *and* in Samaria, *and* unto the uttermost part" (Acts 1:8, KJV). Dave Rohrer, converted while an admiral's writer in the Navy, later headed The Navigators' work for all Europe. The Navy chief who brought him to the Lord was Don Rosenberger, who now directs the Christian Youth Crusade in Washington, D.C. Don's spiritual father, Kenny Watters, now has a responsible part in the work of Wycliffe Bible Translators, giving unreached tribes God's Word in their language. And Kenny was one of the sailors Jim Downing reached and taught several years before on the *West Virginia*.

Thus Jim's spiritual sons of several generations are serving Christ throughout the world, while Jim, retired from the Navy, serves Him at Navigator headquarters. As captain of the U.S.S. *Patapsco*, he was self-appointed chaplain on his ship. On Sunday mornings his crew listened with respect to the gospel message given by their firm, kindly commander who had earned their respect during the week. In over twenty years of soulwinning, Jim has found it pays to attempt first to "win a hearing" for the gospel, and to make disciples of the men who respond.

Some of us have gotten no further than "Jerusalem" with our witness. Some have not even witnessed at home. One key to the answer is the Word. May God help us to feed our own souls daily with it, live it before others as we speak it with the authority of God's messenger—and then train our babes in Christ to follow Him!

Hidden Power

Published in Vision and Venture
August 1954

A young sailor in the United States Navy thoughtfully mulled over a problem. He had known Christ for several weeks now, and the joy of his new life made him long to tell his buddies about Jesus Christ. But how to do it? What should he say? They must hear the Story, but as such a new Christian, how could he tell them? He glanced at the verse cards in his hand. The top one read, "Therefore if any man be in Christ, he is a new creature: old things are passed away; behold, all things are become new" (2 Corinthians 5:17, KJV). That's what had happened; everything was new, and it could be new for *them* too. But how could he explain God's marvelous plan for their salvation?

As he pondered the question, one of his buddies walked by. The first sailor handed him the verse cards. "Will you check me on these? Listen while I quote them." A surprised buddy reached for the cards. As he listened, a reflective look crossed his face. "The wages of sin is death, but the gift of God is eternal life . . ." "Therefore if any man be in Christ he is a new creature . . ." and so on. Each verse seemed to drive straight home to his heart the story of God's wonderful plan of salvation; and before long, he asked the Lord Jesus Christ to come into his life.

Thus, the one who did not know how to witness for Christ found that the Word of God written upon his own heart was the effective instrument in reaching another life.

This lad is one of thousands who have learned the value of having the living and powerful Word hidden in their hearts, that the Spirit of God may use it at a moment's notice to reach a heart for Him.

In fact, it was a series of Scripture verses which I learned for a young people's contest that transformed my own life. I was a 20-year-old lumber truck driver for whom spiritual things held little interest, but rivalry of any kind was a challenge. Because I wanted our side to win the contest, I memorized all of the twenty passages given me—10 verses on salvation and 10 more on how to live the victorious Christian life. Then one day on the way to work, one of the verses flashed through my mind over and over. "Verily, verily, I say unto you, He that heareth my word, and believeth on him that sent me, hath everlasting life, and shall not come into condemnation; but is passed from death unto life" (John 5:24, KJV). In that moment I turned my heart to Christ, taking Him at His Word. Many times since then I have been grateful for those verses which not only made clear to me salvation's plan but taught me what my resources were as a young Christian. The second group of ten verses planted in my heart helped to meet the attacks of Satan in doubt and discouragement and started me on the road to living the life.

God's Word in my heart was so effective in helping me lead my fellow-workers to Christ and in starting them growing in the Christian life that I began to do what I could to help others hide the Word in *their* hearts. A Sunday school class of six high school boys was the start, and before long two hundred boys in our small town had received the Saviour and were carrying pocket testaments, learning verses, applying them to daily life and attending Sunday school and church.

Then began the work among men of the Navy—a work later dubbed "The Navigators" by the men themselves, because they learned how to use the Bible as their chart in navigating the sea of life, with Christ as their Captain. In the score of years that has followed, we have seen countless young men in uniform find the memorized Word of God a help toward victory over sin, a means of witnessing for Christ and of strengthening their life and influence for Him. Not long ago I met a young sailor who had known Christ only four months but had led other men to the Saviour, one of whom had led another who in turn had led another!

It works not only for servicemen, but for others as well. In the three years that we have worked with the evangelist Billy Graham in training personal counselors and following up converts during his city-wide Crusades, individual memory of Scripture has proven most valuable to counselor and convert alike. During the recent Crusade in London, where Pocket Testament League supplied thousands of gospels to new Christians, many letters were received in the follow-up office describing new experiences with God's Word.

Even before the Crusade began, those who attended counselor training classes were using the memorized Word of God to win others to Christ. One counselor was reviewing the verses learned in the "Beginning with Christ" packet when her 73-year-old mother said, "I wish I had that which makes you so happy." After the counselor pointed her to Revelation 3:20 and then to 1 John 5:12 that she might know for certain that she could have eternal life, the elderly matron asked Jesus Christ quite simply to come into her heart. Later when some past deed came to mind, the counselor showed her how 1 John 1:9 gave assurance of forgiveness.

Another counselor who had been converted for several years said that he had never really known victory in his Christian life, but that he was experiencing it now, thanks to having God's Word written on his heart.

A Christian leader who served on the committee sponsoring the Crusade began incorporating into his life the habit of memorizing Scripture and expressed great joy in his new discovery. Many ministers who assisted in the Crusade testified to the blessing that had come to their own lives by this means. One said he had been in Christian work for many years and wondered why he hadn't discovered this secret before.

One who made a decision during the meetings wrote, "I feel that as a Christian I have no excuse for not memorizing the Word of God even in times of rush and illness . . . I have great joy and benefit in learning the verses and there have been various occasions when I was able to pick out one of the verses and pass it on." Another wrote, "I realize now, as never before, the necessity of memorization, that it is as essential as anything else which employs my time."

In London, since the Graham Crusade, 25 to 30 enrollments are being received daily for the Topical Memory System, a correspondence course developed over a period of years. The course teaches in simple fashion the principles of successfully writing God's Word on the heart and gives a series of appropriate verses for the Christian life, topically arranged, on which to begin. Many are finding that memorization of Scripture is not merely an activity for the Sunday school but something that God desires of every Christian.

"And thou shalt love the Lord thy God with all thine heart,
and with all thy soul, and with all thy might. And these words,
which I command thee this day, shall be *in thine heart*."
—Deuteronomy 6:5-6 (kjv, emphasis added)

Immutability of God

February 16, 1956

"Art thou not from everlasting, O Lord my God, mine Holy One? we shall not die. O Lord, Thou hast ordained them for judgment; and, O mighty God, Thou hast established them for correction" (Habakkuk 1:12, KJV).

Gang, circumstances change; our situations change; our outlook changes; our dreams change; our ideas are lost in the shuffle; but with God, nothing changes. God has a plan. Before the foundation of the world, God visualized the Cross . . . not a bone broken, men casting lots. The story of the crucifixion was written by men before the Roman Empire came into being. How foolish the prophet must have felt writing such things. Job felt that way: "Who is he that hideth counsel without knowledge? therefore have I uttered that I understood not; things too wonderful for me, which I knew not" (Job 42:3, KJV).

This little earth is going through space; it is going to burn up some day. It is like a garment that gets old . . . it is going to disintegrate. Think of the stars, the Lord made them all. Nothing is going to change. If the weather changes, that doesn't change God. When there are spots on the sun, something cataclysmic has happened. The mathematicians figure there will be storms on the earth in a matter of weeks. God knew it all the time. "Art Thou not everlasting?"

The thing that will stabilize your life is to get your eyes off your circumstances, self, and personal desires and to get your eyes on the God of the universe Who is interested in you and your future, and then rest in this commitment. I see some of you rock continually. One time you are jovial and radiant, and the next time you are different. It is the things that take you off your guard. It is the trials and testings that build the spiritual man.

[Gave illustration of Major Domo and rock strata.]

When Dick Hillis says that we need two missionaries by March, I could let this rock me. I must serenely go on my way without it rocking me. Just like a fish on the bottom of the ocean — they are not rocked by the sea waves.

Moses died, and the Lord spoke to Joshua: "As I was with Moses, so I will be with thee" (Joshua 1:5, KJV). What did Joshua have on you and me? Gang, we have some things on Joshua. Joshua never had a copy of the Old or New Testaments, a concordance, electric lights to study by at night, or central heating. The thing the Lord said was that He was the God of Abraham, Jacob, and Isaac. Sometimes one of the servants would say, "Where is the God of Elijah, Jacob, and Isaac?"

He can do for and through us anything He did for or through these fellows. He was not rocked by earth's circumstances. You are using energy, faith, strength as you watch these little things.

I don't know how many mistakes I make a day. If I let it rock me that I was going to be making mistakes, I could get flustered. The Lord is from everlasting. The Eternal One was and is alive forevermore. Gang, don't be over-elated about some people. Let Him run the show. Put your faith on Him and trust Him.

I know a lot of you kids that say you could stand a job for a month, two months, or three months, but you hope you don't have a job for a year. You know what you are asking? You are asking the Eternal One to give you the job for a year. Our God is in the heavens. He has done whatsoever He has pleased; He is doing whatsoever He pleases; He is going to do whatsoever He pleases. All of the mistakes you make are not going to change His will for your life.

[Illustration of the letter written against Dawson, and the woman who made up a story about him.]

These things taught me much about the Lord. "No weapon that is formed against thee shall prosper; and every tongue that shall rise against

204   Dawson Trotman: In His Own Words

thee in judgment thou shalt condemn. This is the heritage of the servants of the LORD, and their righteousness is of me, saith the LORD" (Isaiah 54:17, KJV). Thy God reigneth. My God reigneth. God runs tiny things. I often think the tiny things are the greatest.

Just relax. Don't try to cook yourself up a good deal. Don't do anything to get something for yourself. You let the Lord do that. Don't try to maneuver; don't use flattery. Don't do anything to attempt to get an edge—or you have had the course. Let the Lord do all the giving of profit. "There is that scattereth, and yet increaseth; and there is that withholdeth more than is meet, but it tendeth to poverty" (Proverbs 11:24, KJV).

Why? The Eternal God isn't shaken by mistakes, sin, or errors of men. He is not turned from His course by lack of materials, money, or any other things. He is watching over you. He has your future at heart.

Discipleship

Published in Park Street Spire, *vol. 2, no. 3*
June 1956

Nothing Is Yours Until You Can Give It Away

The first words of commandment given in the Bible are, "Be fruitful and multiply." In the beginning God created Adam and Eve in His own image. And God wanted more Adams, but He didn't want to create them as He had created Adam. So He gave man a part. He said, "Be fruitful and multiply," so that there will be over 2,000,000,000 people on the earth in 1956. And all God needed was two. All He needed was a beginning.

When God made man, He made him in His own image to love and worship Him. He created man for His own pleasure. And the plan was wrecked. But God had another plan in reserve. There was to be a last Adam. Jesus Christ was to be that One. And every believer is made in His image. This is the beautiful plan of God.

Christians are born into God's family in somewhat the same series of events as a human is born. First, the incorruptible seed of the Word of God is sown in the heart. Man believeth. And here is a new little creation.

Here is a little baby with two hands, two ears, two eyes, a nose and a mouth. It can't even recognize its own mother, yet. It can't do anything, yet. It can't even hold a rattle, yet. But in those tiny fingers, in those lips lie the potential of a great musician. But that has got to be claimed. And every true believer born into the family of God has the potential of being a reproducer.

Herein lies a tragedy. We lead a soul to Christ, and because that soul is not followed up and taught, his potential is lost. He is sterile. And all the seed that might have come to him is lost.

15 1/2 Years to Evangelize World

In the New Testament, the Gospel was carried from lip to lip, from life to life. If one person taught another for six months, and those two went out and won two more, and those reproduced, do you know how long it would take to evangelize the world? Fifteen and a half years! And do you know how many would have heard the Gospel? 2,176,000,000 — all the people in the entire world with the exception of the three-year-olds and under. Fifteen and a half years!

We think we have to have a dozen Billy Grahams. No. That isn't God's plan. Why under heaven cannot we see the fact that every true believer is a potential reproducer!

We are constantly looking for new methods and materials. If the printing press, the radio, television, and all the things we think we need today had been essential to the evangelization of their generation, Jesus Christ would have given these things to the disciples. Right?

Challenge 2%, Decision 5%, Follow-Up 95%

I work with a group called The Navigators. I am usually introduced, "This is Daws Trotman of The Navigators. The Navigators, as you know, is a memory system."

We began about twenty-four years ago in a little town. After three years of working with the boys of that community, we saw the whole football team come to Christ. It was a big day when the thirty-third member of that team came to Christ. We used much the same methods that are now employed by the Young Life Campaign — sitting on the benches with the fellows, umpiring games, or refereeing. And about that time, the Lord laid it on my heart to work with a little older type of men.

I find in the Word that the Lord Jesus worked with all ages—children and old folks and everyone. Yet He confined a good deal of His effort to a dozen men old enough to make decisions and yet yet impressionable. So we formed what was known as the Minute Men. And as we worked among people, one thing stood out to me over and over again. People want to be challenged.

We tried to get decisions. And we got them. Yet, as I took inventory and checked back, I found a year later that those decisions that had been made hadn't been followed through. I reached the conclusion in talking to many that perhaps challenge might be considered 2%, getting the decision 5%, getting that decision carried out 95%.

Out of this discovery The Navigators was born. Our purpose—follow-up. Now follow-up is a poor word, and yet I believe that it is as near as we can come to the meaning. Follow-up simply means to stick with a convert until he is a disciple. To teach him all you know about the Bible so that he can then go out and teach someone else all he knows.

Primarily, The Navigators is a service organization. We serve many groups. We serve Charles E. Fuller's broadcast, World Vision, we work in Korea, Formosa, Vietnam, Hong-Kong, the Philippines, with various college groups, with the Young Life Movement, the Pocket Testament League and various other groups. The largest work we have is the follow-up with Billy Graham.

Methods Can Become Monstrosities

When we first started out, we had a good many battles. I got one fellow from a battleship. I spent three nights every week for several months teaching him all I knew of the Bible. I got him to get one more. Each of those got one more. Pretty soon there were enough for a Bible class. So they had a Bible class. Pretty soon more fellows on the ship got saved. Then they found that while they taught the older Christians, they lost out with the newer ones. So they formed two Bible classes—one for the older and one for the younger Christians.

Later we started a Sunday morning service to get the fellows to stay to church. We co-operated with the chaplain and we pulled together on the ship to do a better job. Then we found we had enough popularity to get permission to announce over the ship's loudspeaker a popular Bible class. It was more or less evangelistic. Then we formed a personal workers class for fellows who didn't know how to win souls. Then we found we had enough Christians to make a Gospel team. And we began to have regular prayer meetings.

Before long, other battleships got wind of the activity, and they wanted everything the first battleship had. And pretty soon this plan was devised: five Bible classes, one Gospel team, twenty-one prayer meetings. Any deviation from that plan wouldn't produce results!

Then the Lord began to break it up. We discovered that the first three or four fellows we worked with were really the only ones that paid off. The others seemed to disappear. Why? We made right there a wonderful discovery, and I thank God for it. We found that when we lost touch with the individual and became large enough to be a class, we were no longer discipling. As long as one man had to talk with and teach one man alone, we grew.

I went through the Gospels and I found this: "Jesus *and His disciples.*" Jesus healed, He taught, He took children in His arms, but always "and His disciples." You can't imagine Jesus Christ being all day with His disciples—twelve of them—walking down the dusty roads without one saying, "Why shouldn't we do thus and so?" and "What did you mean by this?" There was a personal man-to-man contact; there was the Paul-Timothy relationship.

I believe this is the great missing link today in Christianity both at home and abroad.

They Had Every Excuse

People aren't getting the job done because they always have some excuse. When I was in Germany for the Graham meetings, they brought up every single excuse.

"We don't have much money."

Jesus sent His disciples out without purse and without script.

"We only have the New Testament. We don't even have a copy of the Old."

The disciples didn't even have a copy of the New.

"We don't have enough tracts, and books, and commentaries in the German language."

The disciples didn't have copies of these.

"We don't have the necessary transportation."

The disciples once had to borrow a burro.

"But what about illiteracy?"

You were illiterate when you were born, but that didn't stop your parents!

"But you don't know what it's like to live in an occupied country."

When the Lord sent out the twelve, they lived in an occupied country.

There is always an excuse! But there *is* no excuse!

They Hadn't Seen It Done

I went with Billy Graham to England. I was there a couple of years before he went for his big campaign. Billy sent me there to set up a training program for personal workers in the London area. My job first of all was to hold all-day sessions with groups of ministers. This frightened me. I was an American and these were Englishmen!

I went to a group on Monday, another on Tuesday, another on Wednesday, etc. I talked. Then they asked questions. The idea was to sell these ministers on the idea of getting their people to join training classes for personal work at the Graham campaign. Our emphasis was not just on getting decisions, but on getting each convert studying the Word and bringing him to the place of full stature in Christ.

But do you know the biggest problem we had with those ministers? It wasn't that we were Americans, after all. It was that they just didn't believe God could do it. They hadn't seen it done. They didn't believe it could be done.

They said, "But how many people do you want?"

And I said, "We want at least fifteen hundred in the city of London."

And do you know, almost without exception, you would hear little snickers going all over the room. And they came to me afterwards and said, "Mr. Trotman, you are in *London!*"

So we said, "You tell your people this, and you get them to volunteer."

Well, they did. And do you know how many showed up? Twenty-nine hundred! And they sat week after week after week as our men spoke in their churches. They had to wear overcoats during those January meetings it was so cold in the buildings. And the steam would come out of their mouths. And the people came. It was necessary to stop every twenty minutes or so and let the people stand up and exercise to get the warmth back in their bodies, and they sat for an hour and a half. Twenty-seven hundred the first night. Twenty-eight hundred the second night. Twenty-nine hundred the third night.

Now out of those twenty-nine hundred people, we estimated from all that we can find out that over 95% had never led a soul to Christ. Before the Graham campaign was over, every one of those twenty-nine hundred had actually been in the inquiry room and had brought souls over the hump to say "Yes" to Jesus Christ.

The Job Can Be Done

It is so possible in any age to look at the difficulties and measure the possibilities by the difficulties. How much of our whole lives are conditioned by that which we expect because of that which we have seen. When we hear a missionary stand up and radiantly tell what marvelous things God is doing in his field, our hearts are warmed. And we think, "I wonder if God could do that for me in my work."

God can do anything that He wants to do where He can find men and women who will believe Him! The problem is how do we expect

God to do in a large way what we haven't even seen Him do in a small way. This is our problem.

The first thing we do in training a disciple is to show him that God can use him in a little way. And to use him in a little way, he has to be faithful in little things. So expect to start little. Little faithfulness—little fruit. More faithfulness—more fruit. Much faithfulness, much pruning—much fruit. Fruit, more fruit, much fruit. That's the order. That's what He wants. That's what He says He wants.

The chief purpose of the Christian is to glorify His Lord. "Herein is my Father glorified, that ye bear much fruit" (John 15:8, KJV).

Are you studying the Word of God and hiding it in your heart, so that you will have something to give out? Are you giving it out? If not, how can you expect those that you teach and evangelize to do something you aren't doing yourself?

When Jesus sent out the twelve, they were given the job of evangelizing the *world*. They had every single problem that you can imagine—persecution included, death included. Jesus Christ did not give us a job that could not be done. It can be done. If we aren't doing it, why aren't we doing it?

How to Memorize Scripture

H. J. Taylor, president of Club Aluminum Company, was once challenged through John 14:15—"If ye love me, keep my commandments" (KJV). He decided that in order to *keep* them, he had to *know* them. So he bought a red-letter edition of the New Testament and began learning the words of Christ. He memorized the Sermon on the Mount and John 13–17. Every day now he reviews these 225 verses, plus many others. Regarding Scripture memory, Taylor says, "Anything that needs to be done *can* be done."

A lawyer once came to Jesus and asked Him what the greatest commandment was. Jesus answered by quoting from the Old Testament, where these words appear: "Hear, O Israel: The Lord our God is one Lord: And thou shalt love the Lord thy God with all thine heart, and with all thy soul, and with all thy might" (Deuteronomy 6:4-5, KJV). "This," said Christ, "is the first and great commandment" (Matthew 22:38, KJV).

But notice the following verse in the text from which Christ quoted: "AND these words, which I command thee this day, SHALL BE IN THINE HEART" (Deuteronomy 6:6, KJV). The command to memorize God's words is linked to the greatest commandment in the Bible!

To help Christians keep this commandment to memorize God's Word, The Navigators developed the Topical Memory System (TMS). Every year approximately 10,000 people enroll in this correspondence course.

What is the basic purpose for this Scripture memory system? We do not believe that the memorization of a certain number of passages is a sufficient goal if the process is then discontinued. Accordingly, the TMS is not intended to be an end in itself nor a sufficient memory goal. It is intended to provide a well-balanced selection of key and summary passages that may be used as a foundation for a lifetime of successful personal memory work.

From the beginning, the TMS is geared to the ultimate objective that a person will, upon completion of the 108 verses, continue systematically to memorize the Word of God. Experience has demonstrated that a thorough "system," and not merely the issuance of printed verses, is necessary if this objective is to be achieved.

Don Rosenberger, director of our Washington, D.C. headquarters, has a wealth of Bible knowledge though he is just a young man. Formerly a Navy Chief, he accepted Christ in the Admiral's office in Hawaii during World War II. Since then he has written on the tables of his heart — for use in his own life and in the lives of others — over 2,000 passages of the Word of God. Don continues to learn a regular number of new verses each week in addition to reviewing the others.

Evolution of the TMS

The development of the present Topical Memory System has taken a number of years. The first memory course the Lord permitted us to put before His people was printed some 24 years ago. Check-up revealed that only 3 percent of those enrolled made real headway in the course. Only 1 percent won the immediate battle of memory in mastering the given verses, and we are not sure that he continued to memorize after the prescribed verses were hidden in his heart. Evidently, something was wrong.

The passage of time revealed the need for a more convenient way to carry the verses, and some people wanted to select their own verses. The second course met these objectives by issuing folders in which to carry the verses, as well as blank cards and printed instructions. Even among Bible school students, there was only about a 10 percent victory and that was short-lived.

Other attempts were made to solve the problem, but not until 1935 were there anything like satisfactory results. At that time we issued a

Topical Memory System that contained 35 subjects with 3 verses on each subject. It was discovered, however, that even with this improved system largely only those who had continual personal follow-up succeeded. Something was missing! What about those with whom we could not keep up this continual grueling personal follow-up?

The TMS Today

Through the Lord's grace, the present Topical Memory System solved many problems. (1) It offered a better selection of verses. Instead of one or two persons selecting the references for the course, some 50 Christian workers from all phases of Christian activity assisted. (2) An outline for the 36 verses — divided into 6 major topics, each with 6 subtopics — was arranged, and each memory card has its topic printed on it. (3) Much more complete instructions were written. (4) A closer check on the progress of each person enrolled in the course was maintained in our files, and more effective follow-up through the mail was established.

But perhaps the major key contributing most to the success of the present TMS is the fact that we began and have continued to issue it in a series of progressive steps. We withhold the main body of verses, issuing only a portion of them at one time. We make available each step only after the preceding one has been satisfactorily memorized.

At the time of enrollment, the Initial Bible Rations (4 verses) and the Initial Test (12 verses) are sent simultaneously. The latter is enclosed in a sealed envelope and must not be opened until the B Rations have been correctly quoted. Upon completion of the Initial Test, Set 1 is sent with instructions. When the individual becomes eligible for Sets 2 and 3, they are sent one at a time. Explanatory booklets, progress tests, and other helps are also sent with the verses.

Its Benefits and Blessings

People from all walks of life have written to say what a blessing the Topical Memory System has been to them. A *pastor* wrote:

This correspondence memory course is one of the most thrilling adventures of my entire Christian life. I had so completely persuaded myself that I was incapable of memory work that now when I find myself easily remembering the Word, it just simply overwhelms me with spiritual joy. I thank God for the occasion that permitted you to challenge my lagging spirit, and stirred me to this endeavor.

A *missionary* in Mexico confessed:

I never realized the blessing of having the Word hid in my heart so much as I do now that I'm out here alone away from all Christian fellowship. There is much blessing in the reading of the Word and in Bible study, but the memorized Word gives strength and refreshing at times when I can't be doing the others.

A *soldier* explained:

Since entering the Army, I have found a fellowship with God utterly better than anything I have ever known. This has been due to turning my mind to Christ at all times when my mind is not occupied by other things. This has been largely due to Scripture memorization. I have also gained a victory by freedom over past besetting sins. This, too, is due to the presence in my mind of great verses of victory. Also, there are spiritual results. Why? I can speak with authority from Scripture I have memorized.

Objection Overruled!

A familiar phrase heard in our courts today is "Objection overruled." This phrase fits the many people who raise objections in memorizing Scripture, even though they realize the extreme value and importance of doing so. One common objection is: *"I don't have time."*

However, we find time for the things we consider most important. For example, we eat three meals a day! Job said, "I have esteemed the words of his mouth more than my necessary food" (Job 23:12, KJV).

Some people merely "kill time," while others take every opportunity for personal spiritual growth. We can learn to derive value from spare minutes that would otherwise be wasted. How? By carrying the memory pack and reviewing verses while walking from place to place, riding the streetcar, waiting for class to start, standing in line, and so on. "Redeeming the time because the days are evil" (Ephesians 5:16, KJV).

Another objection runs like this: *"I just simply can't memorize."* If a person can train his mind to remember a street address or phone number, he can learn Scripture if he really wills to do so. Spurgeon, a famous British preacher, once said: "There is no limit to what you can do with your memory, if you are only determined to make it your obedient servant."

Establishing proper habits from the start is important. In the beginning, learn a passage correctly word for word. Maintaining a "word perfect" standard pays rich dividends.

Oscar Lowry, who invented a card system in 1898, introduced thousands to the adventure of Scripture memorizing through his book *Scripture Memorizing for Successful Soul-Winning*. He wrote:

> I consider that next to my conversion the greatest blessing that has come to me in this world was when the Lord led me to see the importance of memorizing His Word. I have been able to memorize thousands of Scripture passages. And all this in spite of the fact that at the beginning of my training, I was one of those who said I could not memorize and quote the Scriptures verbatim. Praise God, I was delivered from that delusion!

A promise to claim for His enabling is John 14:26. "He shall teach you all things, and bring all things to your remembrance, whatsoever I have said unto you" (KJV). The Holy Spirit enables us both to memorize and retain the Word. In Isaiah 59:21 the Lord said *He* would put His Word in our mouths.

Some claim: *"I'm too old."* Age is no barrier. Mrs. Huang in Shanghai, China is 80 years old. Already she can quote most of the 108 verses in the course. Another Chinese grandmother learned to freely quote the Gospel of John.

In a memory class in California a woman of 72 and another of 78 finished the Topical Memory System. One of them wrote:

> I'm not very strong, but I'm glad my mind will work. The Bible means much to me. I shall keep on working on the verses until they become as much a part of me as the 23rd Psalm is. I know these 108 verses and their references, but when they become a part of you, there is more joy in meditating on them.

The TMS is designed for those of high school age and over. However, a 9-year-old boy completed it in record time. When grading his last progress test written in a childish scrawl, we found a touching reply to the question "What helped you most in completing this course?" His answer: "Mama and Jesus."

Many raise still another objection: *"Memorizing is for Primaries and Juniors in High School."* The command to memorize was given to *all* believers. Many leaders of missionary organizations and Christian groups have taken and mastered the TMS—Ford Canfield, China Inland Mission overseas director in the Orient; Bob Evans, founder and director of the European Bible Institute; Charles Cooper, former president of the Los Angeles Christian Business Men's Committee; Fred Mitchell, CIM home director in Great Britain; Cliff Barrows, song leader for the Billy Graham Crusades. Also, other members of the Graham team are currently taking the course.

Cliff wrote: "I'd just like to give you my own personal testimony in regard to the blessing that the TMS has been to my heart and life. It's been worth its weight in gold and many times over."

Three Youth for Christ leaders each agreed that Scripture memory was the greatest one thing that ever happened to them next to their salvation! These men are Hubert Mitchell, former director of YFC in India; Dave Morken, YFC director for Japan; and Dick Hillis, director of YFC in Formosa.

"I have difficulty with references" is a widespread objection. Knowing the location of each verse is important. We have discovered a method for mastering the reference location that is quite simple. Once the book, chapter, and verse is memorized, it must be reviewed. To accomplish this most easily, we recommend the "fore 'n aft" rule. Each time you say a verse, repeat the reference before and after. Saying it at the beginning and ending of the quotation makes a double impression.

This also answers the unfounded objection that memorizing a verse removes it from its context. On the contrary, the memorized verse with its reference location serves as a reminder of the context.

Some complain: *"I can learn a verse but soon forget it."* The secret of successful memorization is Review—Review—REVIEW. The time devoted to initially memorizing a verse is of comparatively little value if the verse is not *retained*. Therefore, while acquiring new verses, great emphasis must be placed upon the retention of those previously memorized by an adequate system of review.

Imagine buying a Bible, opening it, and reading from its precious pages the Word of God; then at a later date, opening it to find the print blurred, and then, in a short time, to again open it and find the print completely gone! This illustrates the effect that results from memorizing without reviewing. Although verses are written on the table of the heart, unless there is proper review the impression that was made on the memory will, in a few days or weeks, be blurred or completely gone!

"My son, keep thy father's commandment, and forsake not the law of thy mother: bind them continually upon thine heart, and tie them about thy neck" (Proverbs 6:20-21, KJV). God's Word must be "bound continually" upon the heart! Just as a farmer binds hay with bailing wire, throwing bind after bind around the bundle until it is secure, so are memorized verses to be secured in the heart by continual review.

"For it is a pleasant thing if thou keep them within thee; they shall withal be fitted in thy lips" (Proverbs 22:18, KJV). Note that it is only as we *keep* (retain) His words within that they are made available for instant use by the Holy Spirit.

Although there are several good methods of review, the following plan is recommended:

1. Every day, work on the new verses assigned for the current week. Scores who are memorizing and who have experimented in this field feel that an assignment of 3 verses a week secures best results.
2. Every day, review all verses memorized during the past 7 weeks. We have conducted tests that demonstrate this much review is necessary before a verse is ready to file.
3. At the end of each week, put into a weekly section of your permanent file box the 3 verses that have been thus reviewed for 7 weeks. Review the verses in this section once a week. When they have been thus reviewed for a while, they can be placed in a monthly section until they are ready for the permanent file, which may be arranged topically or by books.
4. Every day, review as many verses in the permanent file as seems best. Several days may be spent on any assigned section of back review, or a different section may be reviewed each day.

"Oh how I love thy law! it is my meditation all the day. Thou through thy commandments hast made me wiser than mine enemies: for they are ever with me" (Psalm 119:97-98, KJV). Notice "they are ever with me." David had learned the secret of having them constantly with him, thus permitting meditation on them any part of or "all the day!" The secret of successful memorization again is Review—Review—REVIEW!

Living Epistles

Finally, live the Word as well as learn it! Strive to meditate on the meaning of each verse. Then, apply the discovered lesson, challenge, or command to your daily life: "Be ye doers of the Word, and not hearers only" (James 1:22, KJV).

It isn't the number of verses you've learned that counts most, but what you are doing with the ones you have memorized. I believe God would rather have a man who knows 50 verses in his heart and is living them than a man who knows 1,000 in his head and doesn't apply them to his life.

Jim Rayburn, director of a nation-wide work among high-schoolers known as Young Life Campaign, once gave the following testimony to the practical effect of the Word in his life.

> Years ago I memorized these two verses, and one morning recently they kept coming to my mind.
>
> "And herein do I exercise myself, to have always a conscience void of offense toward God, and toward men" (Acts 24:16).
>
> "Let nothing be done through strife or vain glory; but in lowliness of mind let each esteem others better than themselves. Look not every man on his own things, but every man also on the things of others" (Philippians 2:3-4).
>
> For a long time I had been troubled about my attitude of heart toward another Christian brother. As the day wore on and I continued almost against my will, to meditate on these two familiar portions that were stored away in my heart through memory, I became convicted of disobedience to the Lord from these verses, and I went quickly to my Christian brother with a humble apology and complete fellowship was instantly restored. It would be impossible to compute the blessing and profit that has come from this one little instance of God using the Word that was hidden in my heart.

Carrying within the very recesses of your heart and mind the living Word of God gives the Holy Spirit, at any moment of any one of the 24 hours of the day, an opportunity to transmit the Word from the Captain of your salvation to fit your own need or the need of anyone to whom you are privileged to minister!

Where to Start

We have had calls for help from many countries in recent years. We have not responded merely with materials, but with men. Memory cards have long been on the market with well-selected, topically arranged verses. However, there is a difference between cards and winning the battle of memory. They are poles apart. We have shown that, along with cards, the Topical Memory System includes a program that helps surmount the many obstacles which ordinarily confront one who sets out to memorize the Word of God.

Although the TMS is handled as an individual correspondence course, many groups have used it successfully. Each person in a group who is interested in launching on a personal memory program should enroll and obtain material for himself so as to have it available for use during the week.

Scripture memorizing is a personal responsibility, but a group working together can challenge, encourage, and spur one another on to victory.

Whether you memorize Scripture through the method described here or some other method is not the major issue. The main point is that God desires each of His children to memorize His Word. "The greatest waste of time is the waste of time in getting started." If you have not already begun to memorize systematically, do so now!

"Let the Word of Christ dwell in you richly in all wisdom; teaching and admonishing one another in psalms and hymns and spiritual songs, singing with grace in your hearts to the Lord" (Colossians 3:16, KJV).

Follow-Up: Conserving the Fruits of Evangelism

Published by Christ for America

Why Follow-Up?

You are in the greatest business on earth—that of bringing men and women into fellowship with Christ and to the place of greatest usefulness in God's marvelous plan. Your church is the heart and local headquarters of this tremendous program of taking the gospel of Christ to every creature and building in each believer a life glorifying to God. The success of this world-wide mission will be the reflection of its success in each community like yours.

We hear anew our Lord's command to take the gospel to the uttermost parts. Realizing this was done by the early church in its generation, let us investigate the reasons for their success. In that day there was no radio, printed page or television to aid in evangelism, yet it was said of the Christians in Rome that their faith was "spoken of throughout the whole world" (Romans 1:8, KJV), and of the Thessalonians, that "from you sounded out the Word of the Lord . . . in every place" (1 Thessalonians 1:8, KJV). The evangelists brought the good news of the gospel to new localities such as Thessalonica and Rome, and saw many respond and turn from idols to serve the living God.

But what had made the mighty impact upon the rest of the world? The transformed lives of the converts, whose influence had spread in widening circles, reaching men and women in every walk of life. These fruitful lives had been built up in the faith by patient, tender care of those able to instruct and equip them for the Christian walk. This is the embodiment of what we commonly term follow-up. To the local body of believers was committed the task of giving the gospel to all the world, and the record shows that it was accomplished (Colossians 1:6).

What significance has this for us as we consider the program of evangelization today? We believe every person in this generation could hear the gospel if the same conditions are fulfilled that brought such results in the first century, and follow-up is given its vital place.

Every member of your congregation who is spiritually healthy should be able to meet his own problems and help care for another. Thus, your personal attention for both—the one helping and the one being helped—may be greatly reduced. However, every member not spiritually strong doubles the responsibility. You must not only care for his own problem but do the work he would be able to lift from your shoulders were he in good spiritual health.

Many pastors are of necessity burdened with the problems and ills of the spiritually sick among their congregation. This forces them to slight their regular duties and put aside the important work of "training the twelve," or the positive ministry of nourishing promising young leadership. The simple application of follow-up will conserve, perpetuate and multiply the fruit of your weeks and months of prayer, visitation, and preaching the gospel. The transformed lives of converts followed up and built into the fiber of the church will begin to bear fruit and continue to thrive and reach others in the community.

In the physical realm, God provides parents for each baby. Giving birth to the child is only the beginning of carrying out the parental responsibility. A baby without proper attention and necessary protection against disease may become a sickly child. The responsibility of the parent is to protect, feed, provide for, guide and train the child. The child must be nurtured to maturity and completely equipped to do and be all that he should as a citizen of his community. The character of the citizen will be the result of the faithfulness of the parent in carrying out his responsibility.

In the spiritual realm, has God anything less wonderful for these who are born new creatures in Christ (2 Corinthians 5:17)? For them all the world is new. They have before them a grand new life with all its potentialities for blessing and profit and use. They can either fall into a nominal Christian existence and be of little help, or an actual hindrance to the cause of Christ, or they can move victoriously into a life of fruitfulness and glory to the Lord. Is it not the responsibility of the spiritual parent, through whom the life was brought into existence, to provide for growth and training of these babes in Christ? You as the pastor have the whole church family upon your heart; you must think of the needs of all, and attend to them in the best measure possible. Yet the answer to filling the initial needs and caring for these young Christians lies with your older Christians and personal workers, those who helped them understand the gospel and come to the place of the new birth. These are the spiritually healthy among your various age groups who can give individual time to individual needs. The baby is not responsible to the parents until it grows a bit older, but from the beginning the parents are responsible to the baby. They must take upon themselves the God-given responsibility of caring for the infant.

God intended that it should be this way. The heavy end of the work of the ministry is to be carried by the people, and not left entirely in the hands of the already overworked pastor. "And He gave some, apostles; and some, prophets; and some, evangelists; and some, pastors and teachers; for the perfecting of the saints, for the work of the ministry, for the edifying of the body of Christ . . . And the things that thou hast heard of me among many witnesses, the same commit thou to faithful men, who shall be able to teach others also" (Ephesians 4:11-12; 2 Timothy 2:2, KJV).

What Is Follow-Up?

Revival may be under way in your community, the evangelistic program may be all you could have expected and more, yet it may lose momentum, wither and die without effective follow-up. You have been busy enlarging the place of your tent (Isaiah 54:2) and lengthening the cords; now it is time to strengthen the stakes, lest your labor be in vain. You have cultivated and prepared the soil through prayer, watered it through personal visitation and publicity, sown the seed of the gospel and have seen tender shoots of new life break through into the light of day. The wonder of new-found joy and faith in Christ will doubtless find expression voluntarily to those around, and the new convert becomes "exhibit A" for the gospel. To this fresh new zeal must be added knowledge, as they reach people with the reality and newness of their testimony that no one else may be in a position to reach.

What then is this vital link called follow-up? Naturally, we understand that it is more than getting the new Christian to read a tract or book of encouragement or instructive material. It is more than getting him to attend church regularly, as essential as this is; for it was to those who were saved and in the church that Paul "sent to know their faith," lest his labor be in vain (2 Thessalonians 3:5, KJV). It covers the whole scope of Christian life and growth following the new birth, the bringing to spiritual maturity and fruitfulness young believers God has committed to one's charge. It is, in effect, spiritual pediatrics, as indicated in 2 Thessalonians 2:7-12, "But we were gentle among you, even as a nurse cherisheth her children . . . As ye know how we exhorted and comforted and charged every one of you, as a father doth his children, that ye would walk worthy of God, Who hath called you unto His kingdom and glory" (KJV).

Effective follow-up begins with effective evangelism. It includes providing conditions for a healthy spiritual birth, digestible food for the spiritual infant, and protection from spiritual disease. Training and correction, encouragement and challenge, instruction and example all contribute toward the goal expressed by the Apostle Paul: "Till we all come in the unity of the faith, and of the knowledge of the Son of God, unto a perfect man, unto the measure of the stature of the fullness of Christ" (Ephesians 4:13, KJV).

Granted, then, that follow-up includes all that parental responsibility entails, toward what tangible goals may we work in seeking to bring the image of Christ into view in the lives of new Christians, and older ones as well? The first and continual need in the physical life is for food: "Brethren, I commend you to God, and to the Word of his grace, which is able to build you up . . . As newborn babes, desire the sincere milk of the Word, that ye may grow thereby" was the advice written to those who had tasted God's grace (Acts 20:32; 1 Peter 2:2, KJV).

Not only is the Word important in building up a Christian life, but so is regular, consistent prayer. Jesus says to those who have come to believe in Him, "Hitherto have ye asked nothing in my name: ask, and ye shall receive, that your joy may be full" (John 16:24, KJV). In fact, prayer and the Word of God are linked inseparably in the life that would be Christ-centered, as pointed out by the Lord Jesus Himself: "If ye abide in me, and my words abide in you, ye shall ask what ye will, and it shall be done unto you" (John 15:7, KJV).

Along with expression of his needs to God in prayer, and personal intake of God's Word, there should be instilled in the Christian the necessity of living in practical application of that Word. Jesus said, "He that hath my commandments, *and keepeth them*, he it is that loveth me" and a little later, "Ye are my friends, if ye do whatsoever I command you" (John 14:21; 15:14, KJV, emphasis added). True fellowship with the Lord Jesus Christ is made possible by faithfulness in carrying out His wishes.

Finally, the one who is thus in fellowship with Christ through the Word, through prayer, through obedience to His known will, will have an effective witness both by life and word to those around him. As he seeks to tell neighbors and friends of his new-found life in Christ, the Word will give him wisdom and give authority to his testimony; prayer will give discretion and open the hearts of those who hear; and an obedient, consistent life will give power to the spoken word. Paul's testimony at Thessalonica was: "For our gospel came not unto you in word only, but also in power, and in the Holy Ghost, and in much assurance; as ye know what manner of men we were among you for your sake" (1 Thessalonians 1:5, KJV). We seek to build on the foundation in the life of each believer a structure which will endure to glorify God. As we help him carry out the command to "grow in grace" (2 Peter 3:18, KJV), we may consider these, then, as definite goals: personal daily intake of God's Word, development of regular prayer habits, consistent obedience and faithful witness to God's grace.

The How of Follow-Up

But how is this important work to follow-up of the young converts to be done? Is the answer merely material to distribute to those who come to Christ? No, it is obvious from the experience of successful follow-up programs, both in the New Testament and out of it, that follow-up is done by *someone*, not by something. Paul wrote to the Thessalonians that he was "night and day praying exceedingly that we might see your face, and might perfect that which is lacking in your faith" (1 Thessalonians 3:10, KJV). To the Romans he wrote, "For I long to see you, that I may impart unto you some spiritual gift, to the end ye may be established" (Romans 1:11 [KJV]). When he had preached the gospel in the cities of Asia Minor under great hardship, and returned to his home church, we read that "some days after Paul said unto Barnabas, Let us go again and visit our brethren in every city where we have preached the Word of the Lord, and see how they do" (Acts 15:36, KJV). Although he wrote to them, he considered personal time with them most necessary for effective building in their lives.

Perhaps yours is a church where a few do the work that many should be doing. This large majority of Christians should have a part, and perhaps would be willing to do so if they but knew what to do and felt qualified to do it. Follow-up is something in which the whole church may have a part.

In getting young Christians established in the Word, no one is more qualified than older Christians who are practicing in their lives the same things. Those who are your personal workers, the ones who may even have had a part in bringing them to Christ, should be among these. But are the new Christians to be encouraged to start daily habits of prayer and Bible study merely by being told? No, they must be shown. The person who seeks to do follow-up must be what he is trying to teach, for the learner will follow the example of the teacher sooner than he will his word. Paul could say, "Those things, which ye have both learned, and received, and heard, and seen in me, do; and the God of peace shall be with you" (Philippians 4:9, KJV). Many Christians who love God and seek to serve Him are yet content to live on the ten to twenty verses of Scripture that they have known for that many years. Is the new Christian who enters your church and the family of God to have such an example set before him, or is he to find Christians who are regularly reading and studying the Word of God and writing it on their hearts? Will he also find those whose own personal prayer habits are regular and effective? The people of the church, who are to be the examples for the young Christians committed to their care, will find the success of their task depends largely upon doing, and being, what they are teaching others to be and do. And how will they begin to do these things? They also must have a pattern to follow, in the officers and in the pastor, whose charge under God is to guide the affairs of the corporate, local body of saints.

How long after the campaign should follow-up be carried on? Let us look again at our purpose in follow-up: "Till we all come in the unity of the faith, and of the knowledge of the Son of God, unto a perfect [mature] man" (Ephesians 4:13, KJV). Borrowing again an illustration from the physical family, the person whose estimated life span is to be threescore years and ten spends approximately twenty years coming to the place of mature usefulness as a member of the human economy. How much time should it be worthwhile to invest, then, in preparation and training in the way of life that is endless? Titus was assured by Paul that "this is a faithful saying, and these things I will that thou affirm constantly, that they which have believed in God might be careful to maintain good works" (Titus 3:8, KJV). Imparting truth, along with being a living embodiment of the truth, is the initial step. But once this is done, a constant vigil must be kept to insure that this truth is carried out daily in the life. It involves correction and instruction, for not only does the human mind forget, but the human will must be challenged to continue steadfast.

Peter, as pacesetter for the saints, was not negligent to put them always in remembrance of the things in which they had already been established. He exhorted them to take heed to the written Word of God, holding it up as a "more sure Word" (2 Peter 1:12-19). Paul too challenged both pastor and people to continue taking in the Word of God. He himself was never satisfied to rest on either the knowledge or accomplishments which were already his. "Brethren, I count not myself to have apprehended . . . I press toward the mark . . . be followers together of me" (Philippians 3:13-17, KJV).

Follow-Up Procedure

Having realized our tremendous responsibility and privilege in building the lives of those who have become new creatures in Jesus Christ, we turn to the practical aspect of what can be done in your situation. What plan may be followed for carrying out follow-up in your local church? Three things are necessary: (1) preparation of certain tools and helps, (2) choice of those who are to do the work, and (3) general procedure to follow.

1. The Tools

The main tools needed will be some simple helps in Bible study and verse memorization designed to meet particular needs in the life of a new Christian. Through personal study he may dig out for himself the answers to needs and questions that arise, and through memory of chosen passages he may carry in his heart at all times the Word of God with which he is to meet temptation.

Another tool you will need to prepare is a simple adequate record system, a means whereby you may know the progress of each member in the materials, and be able to take note of individual needs. As progress is noted regularly, these records can be valuable in calling to your attention those who by their faithfulness are proving themselves trustworthy of greater responsibilities. They may also be used to enable you to note lack of progress where encouragement or challenge is necessary and to see that the cause is investigated.

It is suggested that simple Bible study and Scripture memory courses be employed, the first steps of which may be given the convert immediately upon making his decision. Unless you have such material available, we recommend the "Initial Bible Rations," containing the first verses given to memorize along with helpful information on the use of memorized verses in the new Christian life. The *Introductory Bible Study*, a first Bible study course designed to be completed in approximately a month by the new Christian or older one, is also recommended for showing him an easy-to-follow way to study the Bible.

The pastor should become personally familiar with these materials and will find it extremely helpful to use them himself. This would allow him to anticipate any problems and also would provide him leverage in getting the church leaders and personal workers to do them. And naturally, the personal workers would find it much to their profit to do the work, and in turn would find this a help in recommending it to the new converts personally.

2. Choosing the Workers

When the early church had a special work to do they chose from among them "men of honest report, full of the Holy Ghost and wisdom, whom we may appoint over this business" (Acts 6:3, KJV). The apostles were too busy with the overall ministry to do this specialized work themselves. However, to oversee even the physical task of caring for the needy, they chose men with spiritual depth and testimony of life . . . men like Stephen, whose mighty sermon and martyrdom proved him to be a man who walked with God.

The pastor should, at least three months before the campaign, call together the men and women, including young people, who love the

Word of God, and begin regular instruction classes for them in personal work and follow-up. (Should the pastor not be able to handle this himself, his best qualified man should be committed the responsibility of follow-up captain to carry out the program in the pastor's stead.) Doubtless, ability along these lines will vary much within the group, according to their knowledge of the Word and ability to apply it to the inquirer's needs. From among this group select a few, more able in the Word, those of Acts 6:3 caliber, who will act as head personal workers, whom the others may consult when help is needed. The number of those selected may vary, according to the size of your church, from two to a dozen or more. These head personal workers will also be the key men and women in the follow-up program as it continues. The pastor will need to instruct these key people individually or in a small group, as well as instructing the entire group of personal workers.

This, then, is the basic structure of your personal work and follow-up corps in the church: the pastor (or his appointed substitute), the head personal workers or advisors, and the personal workers themselves.

Various plans may be used for these preliminary instruction meetings, but the main goals to be accomplished are these:

1. Recommend that each personal worker get started in the Bible study and memory program that is to be used for the new converts. It may be interesting and stimulating to report progress in these materials at the regular personal workers meetings or in groups at cottage prayer meetings, and share things of special blessing or interest.

2. Instruction in personal work itself—such things as use of the Word, meeting of individual needs and common excuses, how to meet the problem most directly from the Word, to be sure the inquirer understands the gospel, etc. You may desire to compile lists of "dos and don'ts for personal workers" on helpful practical points.

3. Instruction in inquiry room procedure—what to do during the invitation, and the selection by the head personal workers of an appropriate worker for each one who comes forward.

4. How to give the Initial Bible Rations or other initial material with explanation sufficient to get the convert started in the Word.

5. General instruction in how to lead the new Christian step by step. This will vary as individuals vary in capacity to digest the Word. However, as early as possible the convert should be started in various methods of intake of Scripture and in regular daily prayer time.

3. General Procedure for Follow-Up

As we have seen, effective follow-up actually begins months before the campaign, with the choice and preparation of personal workers and instruction in inquiry room procedure. The clarity and simplicity with which the gospel message itself is presented, both by evangelist and personal worker, also bears directly on the follow-up.

The campaign is in progress. Each one who has made a decision has been given the Initial Bible Rations and the Gospel of John, if these are to be used. The personal worker has turned in to the follow-up office through the head personal worker a decision card completely filled out with name, address, approximate age, kind of decision, and any other information desired. Those who have made decisions for Christ during the previous weeks of visitation evangelism may be recorded in the same way.

The pastor may give the advisors or head personal workers the responsibility of seeing that the proper personal worker is selected for each one who comes forward in the meeting—that is, of same sex and general age group, special workers for children, etc.

The pastor will be responsible to see that each person making a decision, whether in or out of the church meeting, has a worker specially appointed to follow him up. Whenever practicable, this should be the one who helped him in the inquiry room. According to the number of decisions, the pastor may wish to make his advisors or head personal workers the captains of follow-up teams, each consisting of several follow-up workers. These workers will keep their respective captains informed, by whatever record system is used, of the progress of the converts for whom they are responsible. The captains will report to the pastor on the progress of both converts and workers. The pastor may wish to call these captains together for regular fellowship, checkup, working out of problems and reporting on progress. Each captain will be working similarly with several workers, and each worker will be following up one or more converts. With the work thus divided and specific responsibilities given, everyone in the church may be receiving personal help by someone, the pastor and leaders may be made aware of any particular needs, and the ones doing the work will be challenged by their responsibility to keep moving ahead.

We have said, "Everyone in the church may be receiving personal help." So far we have made no mention of those who were not qualified as workers, and hence not included in the set-up just outlined. For any among these others who desire help, provision could be made for the workers to get them started in the Bible study, helping them *one by one* as they are able to take them on without neglecting their first responsibility—the new converts. Thus these others in the church could be preparing themselves for usefulness as personal workers in the future.

You will find that when each member of your church is faithfully digging into the Word day after day on his own and memorizing it, your problems will be reduced and you will have time to give to the positive side of your ministry. "And now, brethren, I commend you to God," Paul told the elders of the Ephesian church, "and to the Word of His grace, which is able to build you up, and to give you an inheritance among all them which are sanctified" (Acts 20:32, KJV). This building process can be going on every day in the life of every member of your church.

This plan is logical in theory, but does it work? Yes, it does work, and is working now in churches very much like yours. One outstanding example is a large West Coast church whose pastor had no more time than the average pastor with a large membership and a wide ministry, not only in the local church but in affairs of the denomination at large. Seeing the need of his people to get into God's Word for themselves, he gave some twenty-two capable, consecrated and willing members of the church the responsibility of leadership. Each of these led a small group of five to a dozen in the use of the same Bible study and Scripture memory materials that the leaders used. To personalize the training of the twenty-two leaders, the pastor or his key man spent special time with a half dozen, who in turn were in a position to spend time with the other leaders, thus completing the chain and making possible individual contact with any who desired or needed it. Today, two years from the inception of the follow-up program, over two hundred in the church are actively engaged in personal daily study of the Bible on their own. These report individually or in small groups weekly, and reach out in ministry to the strategic university area of which they are a part.

A strong follow-up program is as necessary to your church for maintenance of normal health and growth as adequate nutrition and medical care are to the family. As you build solidly in the lives of those who are the central force of the local assembly, the church grows in strength and number, becoming an academy of strong, rugged soldiers of the Cross whose multiplied influence can eventually reach to every nook and corner of the world.

God is permitting us to see the beginning of a new era in the ministry of the church. Before long we may rejoice that the final command of our Lord Jesus Christ has been completely carried out.

About the Contributors

KEN ALBERT is the director of the Southeastern Indiana Baptist Association and the associate pastor of evangelism and discipleship at Eastern Heights Baptist Church in Jeffersonville, Indiana, where he lives with his wife, Shawna, and his two boys, Jerome and Caleb. Ken regularly leads conferences on evangelism and discipleship, and over the past few years, he has preached in more than forty churches in ten states. He has served as either senior or interim pastor and has helped plant several churches. Ken earned an MDiv from Golden Gate Baptist Theological Seminary and a ThM from The Southern Baptist Theological Seminary, where he is nearing completion on a PhD in evangelism.

》》》》

SUSAN FLETCHER is the historian and archivist for The Navigators. In this role, she cares for the Dawson Trotman letters and journals that appear in this book. Susan has written articles for *The Church of God Evangel*, *The Encyclopedia of Antislavery and Abolition*, and *The Encyclopedia of American Reform Movements*. In addition to her duties for The Navigators, she also serves on the Colorado Springs Historic Preservation Board and is a featured speaker on local history throughout the region. Susan received her MA in public history from Indiana University–Purdue University Indianapolis. She currently lives in her beautiful hometown of Colorado Springs, Colorado.

» » » »

DOUG HANKINS is the discipleship pastor at Highland Baptist Church in Waco, Texas, and is a PhD candidate in historical theology at Trinity Evangelical Divinity School. Doug has contributed articles for *The New Dictionary of Theology* and *The Gospel Coalition Blog* and has written book reviews for various academic journals. Doug received both a BA and MDiv from Baylor University. When not coordinating Sunday school classes and small-group meetings, he divides his time between reading books, listening to music, and playing basketball. He is married to Natalie and resides in a suburb outside of Waco. You may follow Doug on twitter@doughankins.

NAVESSENTIALS

Voices of The Navigators—Past, Present, and Future

NAVESSENTIALS offer core Navigator messages from such authors as Jim Downing, LeRoy Eims, Mike Treneer, and more — at an affordable price. This new series will deeply influence generations in the movement of discipleship. Learn from the old and new messages of The Navigators how powerful and transformational the life of a disciple truly is.

Meditation
by Jim Downing
9781615217250 | $5.00

Advancing the Gospel
by Mike Treneer
9781617471575 | $5.00

Laboring in the Harvest
by LeRoy Eims with Randy Eims
9781615216406 | $10.99

To order, go to **www.NavPress.com** or call **1-800-366-7788**.

NAVPRESS
Discipleship Inside Out™